The Price of Women

The Price of Women

DAVID ALLEN

JARROW PRESS, INC.
NEW YORK
1971

Published and distributed by Jarrow Press, Inc.

First Edition

Library of Congress Catalog Number: 75-150601
ISBN Number: 0-912190-04-3

Printed in the United States of America

Acknowledgments

This book utilizes and synthesizes the work of many men, none of whom is responsible for the uses to which I have put his work. The author accepts full responsibility for the conceptual framework within which these various contributions will be found. My special thanks to Lionel Tiger of Rutgers University and Frank Beach of the University of California for their efforts on my behalf.

Contents

The Price of Women

Introduction

This book is being written at a time of revolutionary challenge to all authority: authority in government, in business, in religion, and in marriage. This means that all four cornerstones of our civilization—the state, the job, the church, and the home—are being simultaneously shaken by criticism. They have been so shaken before—but usually one at a time. That they should all be shaken at once is unusual in history; that is why the criticism seems so devastating.

In addition, we also have a generation gap so wide as to portend nothing less than a turning point in history. Some people believe that this is the moment of Armaggedon for the American Dream, that another Dark Age is at hand—this despite the fact that the young generation is so intensely idealistic that the American Dream should burn more luminously than ever before.

But there are also those who have lived long enough to judge this period in perspective, who find it not nearly as frightening as the Great Depression. These ancients believe that, having weathered that time of troubles, we may weather this one too, and emerge from it stronger than ever.

Still, the majority fear decline. In the realm of the state, vast numbers bemoan what seems to be a permanent loss of the democratic process. Politicians seem to be unresponsive to the popular will, though hypersensitive to every nuance of special interest. Yet many of the critics would themselves abolish the Bill of Rights.

The church is under attack from no external enemy; but the forces of reform within it are so extreme that they may disrupt and alter the institution beyond recognition.

In the world of work we have, some time ago, begun to admit that the machine is a juggernaut running wild.

In these three realms of life great changes are obviously needed, both for their own sake and to relieve the pressure on the man-woman relationship. As a result of the buildup of tension all around, there has been some spill-over into this fourth realm, and once again the women are sending up distress signals in the form of demands for more equality. One cannot help but reflect that one has heard that song before.

In this book, it will be my central thesis that there is indeed something wrong with the basic relationship between the sexes, something that urgently needs correcting, and insofar as this is true the current feminist cry for reform has some legitimacy. But I take issue with the feminist diagnosis of just what is wrong, and with the feminist prescription for cure. What is needed is not more equality or greater freedom *for* the female, but more responsibility *from* her.

Because there once was a time when the female suffered injustice and had legitimate grievance—which was redressed—the distaff side has fallen into a bad habit: Whenever pressure is felt from any source whatever, the female responds with a conditioned reflex, and automatically cries "injustice."

One of the points I should like to make here is that this response is old hat. These are new times with new conditions; the old conditioned response is inappropriate now, germane as it may have been to another stimulus in another era. To approach a new war with the weapons and tactics of the old, is to invite defeat. Indeed, to approach the new crisis with the old outlook may make it impossible even to find the battlefield.

But change is clearly needed, and a dazzling opportunity has opened up for women to move into an entirely new dimension of personal growth. The new possibilities have been there for several decades, but so far the female has failed to take advantage of them. She has muffed her chances mostly because she wanted to attain all the prerogatives of the masculine way of life while avoiding its attendant disadvantages, and she has attempted to do away with the feminine disadvantages while holding on to her advantages. Because of her reluctance to pay the price of maximizing her potential, she is blind to the opportunity under her nose and instead cocks her ear to the enchanting sound of a distant drummer. It is my intention to refocus her attention on the possibilities that have long been at hand. Though that which is near usually suffers from a lack of glamour compared to that which is far, it does have the virtue of being accessible.

Old Approaches and New Departures

I have agreed that there is something wrong with woman's lot that warrants action, but I would like to attach a rider to the effect that there is something wrong with man's lot as well. It is just possible that what is wrong with woman's lot may be connected with what is wrong with man's. It behooves us to examine them together rather than in separate compartments.

If we put men, women, and children into the same picture we shall be able to get a look at the total emotional economy, just the way we view the money economy. We shall be able to observe the effect of one dynamic force upon another. It can readily be seen that the emotional economy seeks dynamic equilibrium, as does the money economy. It can suffer instability and extreme fluctuation, and experience soaring dislocations. One part can prosper at the expense of another. It can have rich members and poor members.

In such a total picture we have objective criteria for distinguishing between good and bad change: Good change *increases* dynamic equilibrium; bad change *decreases* it. Every change will have a corresponding cost. With such a model we can maximize profits for all, and avoid favoring one group at the expense of another, provided we do not push the use of it too far. Heretofore, when examining the power relationship between the sexes, we have not had such a model. Changes in roles were made haphazardly, with no consideration of the impact of change of one member's role, upon another; no evaluation of cost or profit; and no thought concerning who paid the cost and who got the profit.

For example, the outcome of the first feminist revolt was that society acceded to women's demands without considering how they would affect the emotional economy. In retrospect, we can see that fortunately the overall emotional economy was somewhat improved. What men lost as men they more than regained as persons in a society in which dynamic equilibrium was radically improved. By good luck, therefore, we got away with a shortsighted change.

But since that time further historic changes have altered the balance of forces within the emotional economy. Costs have risen sharply for men, with no corresponding increase in benefits. Men are clearly in the area of "marginal returns," putting in more and more for less and less. At the same time profits to women and children have risen, with no additional inputs from them. The system has moved into disequilibrium.

Therefore, in the face of the new feminist demands for more equality, we want to know what the cost will be and how it will be allocated. If increased benefits *to* women are to be paid for *by* women, the change is possible. But if the cost is to be borne by men, the current disequilibrium will obviously be increased. We may want to consider other alternatives. Possibly we may want to shift some of the existing costs to women, with no corresponding increase in benefits. But we must not get into a rut, and assume automatically that more of the hair of the dog that bit us is the proper remedy. The really right remedy might be very different. Certainly the last remedy that was applied did not prove effective for very long, though at the time it was thought to be a permanent cure.

The first generation of women emancipated from legal, political, and economic serfdom—which I call "structural" restrictions— is still alive. It was only yesterday that the feminist revolution was thought to be won. The female cut her hair and skirts, bought a pack of cigarettes on the way to the voting booth, and after pulling the lever enrolled in a typing school and entered the world of work. What more is left? Did the first generation of feminists fail to do the job completely, or have changed circumstances called forth new complaints? Are we hearing the prophetic voice of Deborah, or is the voice of the shrew once more being heard in the land? The best way to tell is to listen, but that is not easy, because an incredible amount of transmission emanates from the neo-feminist quarter. It is difficult to discriminate, especially since the new feminists already display a generation gap. Arbitrarily, I am selecting the founders of the new feminism as the chief spokesmen to whom I will address myself, though there are many others more vocal now. It is the elder ideologists who have laid down the party line which the younger generation is now applying; and, with one exception, the younger women have not added anything basically new to the corpus of feminist thought. Simone de Beauvoir, the French authoress of *The Second Sex,* Ashley Montagu, the anthropologist author of *The Natural Superiority of Women,* and the indomitable Betty Friedan, authoress of *The Feminine Mystique* and founder of NOW (the National Organization for Women) are the principal architects of the new movement. They have bred a generation smarting with a sense of injustice; but the new voices tend to be repetitive, and none of them has yet made any fundamental ideological contributions to feminist thought—with the exception of Kate Millett, authoress of *Sexual Politics.* She has an insight which expands our field of vision, but has failed to separate the companion insight and the conceptual apparatus in which to place both, which would have allowed thinking in this field to reach its inevitable conclusion. At the appropriate place, I will supply that lack here.

But basically I am directing my attention to the ideological thrust of feminism, not to its organization and practical politics.

I also pay heed to writers like Myron Brenton, author of *The American Male,* and Vance Packard, author of *The Sexual Wilderness,* neither of whom is a feminist in the sense that Montagu is, but both of whom are sympathetic to some of the feminist demands. Men of this type write from a masculinist standpoint but have a highly developed sense of social justice, which is troubled by feminist claims of injustice. This makes them favorably disposed towards the feminists, without going along all the way with their demands for equality. Like Millett, these writers are hampered by lack of a conceptual framework in which to place their intuitive knowledge. Once this conceptual framework is erected, they will be able to solve their dilemmas. As of now, however, they counsel men to abandon the old definition of masculinity in favor of a broader one, more in keeping with man's actual present position as a flunky in the world of work. Naturally the newer definition of masculinity would, in practice, cede to the feminists what they demand.

Apart from those men, one may search libraries far and wide

for a male writer who will go further and defend men's ancient prerogatives. They will not find one, short of going back to the Victorians. As far as male authors of books go, the feminists have been legitimized by default. Only a few newspaper columnists, in a passing paragraph here and there, have dared to intimate that the new feminists' claim to equality may not represent the last word in social justice. Among the rest of the liberal-democratic-university intellectuals, there has been either tacit capitulation or complacency.

But capitulation is a tragic mistake, and complacency is dangerous. The new feminists are having a decisive effect on the younger generation of college-bred females. The end result of this effect will be to make man's life more miserable than it already is, unless he bestirs himself. Fortunately, the most recent ideological development of the feminist movement makes a male defense of selfish interest not only permissible but mandatory.

The elder generation contended that women were historically the first group against whom bigotry was directed and that they therefore have a more ancient claim to social justice than the more recently disenfranchised groups, such as Jews or Blacks. The younger generation of feminist propagandists have elaborated upon this theme and reiterated it to the point where it has become persuasive to large segments of the female "class." But now that women have asserted their "class interest" as females as against the class interest of males, men need no longer feel guilt at asserting their own selfish class interests. This decision has been taken out of our hands, and the onus rests upon women. Men are now forced to take issue with the feminists on a "class" basis; this is a fortunate development, for up to this time the structure of debate—and nondebate—has allowed women to present a monstrously one-sided case. Now that they have pushed their cause into a class context, men can respond to it within this context and at last bring the whole case into court.

To the neo-feminist spokesmen and their male fellow-travelers I propose to make a masculinist rejoinder. That is, I intend to oppose the female class interest with the male class interest, just as selfishly as the feminists do. Where possible I propose to do this with new arguments and facts, of which plenty have accumulated since the first male chauvinist put pen to paper. But I do not propose to abandon old arguments that are still valid simply because they are old; to be old is not necessarily to be passé. But I do intend to bring old arguments up to date and refurbish them in the light of new scientific developments. Today we *need* a Men's Liberation Movement to oppose the Women's Liberation Movement—to defend the masculine class from the feminists and to defend it from males with a penchant for new fashions in ideas simply because they are new. We need it to defend ourselves from those whose education has outstripped their intuition, and allows them to entertain ideas as true simply because they have not been effectively opposed.

In pleading men's case, our class interest, I do not pretend to a posture of objectivity while at the same time pleading a special cause, as the feminists do. The reader should realize I am an advocate, writing a brief, to plead a client's case. We have had an avalanche of partisan pleading in favor of neo-feminist demands. A masculinist reply is clearly in order.

I am assuming, perhaps unfairly, that the neo-feminists truly believe that there is nothing sound to be said in defense of a masculinist position. If I am wrong, I apologize. If I am right, and they will hear me out through courtesy alone, I think I can display some evidence which they have not fully considered, and which cannot be brushed aside as the rhetoric of masculine prejudice. It may strengthen their tolerance if they understand that I also am a political liberal, not a conservative. In my youth I was an ardent Roosevelt champion. My first presidential election vote was cast for Truman over Dewey. I supported Adlai Stevenson over Kennedy as well as over Eisenhower. I also favored Eugene McCarthy over Hubert Humphrey. In fact, until I began thinking about modern feminism, I never quite understood why some people were conservative. Thanks to this study I know, at last: A conservative is a person who has something to lose by change. A liberal is one who has something to gain.

The first thing to be done is to restate the Gospel of Neo-Feminism according to its new Apostles. Right off the bat I am open to charges of distortion, misquotation, and setting up straw men for easy demolition. But the dialog can hardly proceed without it.

According to Betty Friedan, who has worked out the history of modern feminism in fine detail, the battle for feminine freedom seemed to be won in principle by 1920, when the right to vote had been achieved. The mopping up operations were still enormous, but a threshold had been reached and passed. If anyone doubted it, they had only to compare the prewar woman with the short-skirted flapper that emerged in the roaring twenties. (Note that every time woman takes a step forward, she hikes her skirt a little higher, as though publicly symbolizing that access to the treasury will now be a little easier.)

The generation that reached adulthood in the 1920's and 30's rushed out of the house to work with a will. Those who lagged behind were dragged out during the worker shortage of World War II.

Then the boys came home, and Rosy the Riveter patriotically shed her long pants and welder's apron for skirts and retreated to the kitchen. At first this looked like a temporary tactical maneuver to help men get reestablished, after which she would infiltrate the work world again. But as time elapsed it became apparent that this was not a tactical retreat but a full scale escape. Rosy the Riveter was abandoning the beachhead her grandmother and mother had purchased at so dear a price, and was voluntarily retiring to the slavery of domesticity.

An explanation had to be found for such a monumental reversal, and resourceful Betty Friedan found one that left feminist values intact: The retreat was not voluntary at all! *Men* were the real culprits—more particularly, magazine editors and market-researchers who were men. The moment these veterans of foreign wars got back into positions of power, they began undermining their benefactors by reversing previous editorial policy. The career girl image was thrown out unceremoniously, in favor of the housewife image. The former was a direct competitor for the male editor and he could easily rationalize her as a neurotic. Whether or not the male editor was being honest or dishonest with himself, he was an expert propagandist for his prejudices. Such men even shook the faith in themselves of the career girl editors, who experienced self-doubt and guilty misgivings over leading a whole generation of women astray. They repented having led others as well as themselves out of the paths of righteousness and into the path of the sinful imitation of men.

By sheer accident, the mental perturbations of the male market-researchers lent support to the male editors. They discovered that the career girl was not much of a target for the appliance industry, whereas the homemaker could be sold over and over again. This being the case, the career girl image obviously had to go. Neither the male editor nor the male researcher were consciously conspiring, but each served the other's purposes by joining in discarding the career girl image. Thus was a revolution wrought by the caprice of the marketplace!

One cannot quarrel with Betty Friedan over this bit of historical research, since she is the expert on the subject. It sounds just insane enough to be true. We are only beginning to understand the extent to which modern history has been made by ad agencies rather than by men with high historical purpose. But one can question her interpretation of just why the tidal wave of feminism was so easily reversed. How was it possible for the imagemakers to win so easily? How could they capriciously and haphazardly accomplish that which previous generations of devout male reactionaries could not? After all, this generation is the living witness to the fact that the whole establishment apparatus cannot maintain a policy which goes against the grain of the people. We have seen a mere handful of intellectuals rout the establishment and turn the majority against the war in Vietnam. How then was it possible for featherweights like popular magazine editors to drive women out of the factory and back into the kitchen—*unless it was with woman's cooperation?*

The answer is simple, but it is not one which the neo-feminists are likely to see or admit, as it lies in the area of their major blind spot. The male imagemakers couldn't have pulled it off without female cooperation, and did, in fact, have that tacit cooperation. They had coincidentally told women exactly what women had wanted to hear—that woman's place is in the home. These ingenious sophisticates had handed women on a silver platter one of the most perfect cover stories of the ages! During the twenty-five years that women had been working, they had quietly discovered something they hadn't known before: They didn't like to work. They did like to be supported. This, however, they could not publicly admit without making fools of themselves. Now men had handed them the perfect excuse to return to the kitchen without having to face the horselaughs. It was exquisitely opportune.

The first generations had been lured into the world of work by their leaders with the promise of freedom from domestic serfdom through exciting "careers." What they actually discovered was that they had exchanged an easy form of serfdom for a harder one! Seeking "careers," they had instead found "jobs." Seeking "freedom," they had won "responsibilty." When they compared the past with the present, they reached the conclusion which any sensible person would reach—that the world of work involves drudgery, is tensely competitive and uptight, and just as boring as the home. But home was not tensely competitive and uptight, and one could stop for a leisurely cup of coffee and

postpone the laundry until another day. Once women realized
they had been had, they did exactly what men would do if they
had the chance: they bailed out.

This obvious insight—that women marry as much to avoid
work as for anything else, is open to all men and women whose
minds have not been overburdened by too much theory. It is an
inflammatory one when publicly pronounced, and can be expected to generate a good deal of heated denial; but when expressed in private conversation it is widely accepted as quite normal. I shall develop it more fully later on. It forms part of a
much more inclusive principle which the neo-feminist leaders
have not yet faced or adequately informed their followers about—
the principle that there can be no freedom without responsibility.
The greater the freedom demanded, the greater the responsibility
that must be accepted.

The fact that this relationship between freedom and responsibility has not been clearly presented to women today, goes far to
explain why so many intelligent and idealistic young women
have been misusing their resources in feminism, rather than entering the wider field of politics. Many of those who automatically
assume that they have been cheated and clamor for justice, would
be mute if they fully understood the price of equality with men.
It will be one of my tasks to clarify that issue for them. In doing
so, I am aware that this will be the first time American women
will be publicly asked to consider the question in its entirety.
Both past and present feminist leaders have talked about freedom or equality alone, completely divorced from responsibility.
It is about time they considered the concepts jointly. Recognition
of the price man has been paying for his dominance over woman
is long overdue. That price tag reads, *full responsibility for her
person and complete denial of his own spontaneity in the process.*
It is a stiff price. The price of full emancipation for women will
be—*total responsibility for themselves,* and, of course, the resultant
loss of spontaneity that such responsibility entails. That, also, is
a stiff price. It is well worth weighing.

But this lacuna in woman's understanding is not her only blind
spot, despite her vaunted intuition. Over the generations since
Mary Wollstonecraft first raised her voice against the dominion
of men, two themes have repeatedly led women upon the rocks.
The first, that the male was a superior creature whom the female
should emulate, led women to remedy deficiencies by adopting
the masculine role as their own—an attempt doomed to failure.

The second, that male dominion follows from the muscle of the evil male, who uses his superior strength to enslave the weak but good female, still befuddles feminine thinking. Men neither conspired to hold women down, or succeeded in doing so by virtue of their superior strength. Every erg of energy man devoted towards subduing the female was matched by an equal contribution from the female toward the same end. Male dominion was not created by man alone but by woman as well; it was the joint effort of the two that created the system of male domination and female subordination.

But the feminists do not believe that the woman was as much responsible as the man. They will admit to the woman being, as de Beauvoir says, "a willing accomplice," but they insist that this was minor and unwitting. They present a united front in maintaining that there is no biological basis whatsoever for male domination. With varying degrees of emphasis, they believe the division of society into dominant male and subordinate female to be a purely social construct of man's making, enforced by his superior muscle power. As such, they maintain, it is unfair and unjust and, in a supposedly ethical age, should be discarded and replaced by equality.

They appear to be untroubled by certain obvious questions. Why, for example, if there is no biological basis to female subordination, do most societies display this prejudice? Among the several thousand societies known to anthropologists, there has never been one in which the sexes were equal, or one in which man was subordinate. Chance alone should have dictated such a development, if there were not something consistently working against it. The feminists are silent on this matter. Neither have they ever asked why a woman wants to "look up to a man," or why, before a blind date, she instinctively wonders whether the man is taller than she. Why should a woman considering herself an equal want to look up to a man, spiritually, emotionally, or physically? These wishes imply a deep-rooted need for subordination, which was put there by nature, not by nurture.

Simone de Beauvoir goes further than other feminists in admitting that women is not only an accomplice to her subordination, but that the sexes have crucial biological differences which express themselves at higher levels of neural organization. She says:

> "On the average, she is shorter than the male and lighter, her skeleton is more delicate, and the pelvis larger . . .;

her connective tissues accumulate fat and her contours are
thus more rounded than those of the male. . . . . Muscular
strength is much less in woman, about two-thirds that of
man; she has less respiratory capacity, the lungs and trachea
being smaller. The larynx is relatively smaller, and in consequence the female voice is higher. The specific gravity of
the blood is lower in woman and there is less hemoglobin;
women are therefore less robust and more disposed to anemia
than are males. Their pulse is more rapid, the vascular system less stable, with ready blushing. Instability is strikingly
characteristic of women's organization in general. . . .
  "Woman is weaker than man; she has less muscular
strength, fewer red blood corpuscles, less lung capacity; she
runs more slowly, can lift less heavy weights, can compete
with man in hardly any sport; she cannot stand up to him
in a fight. To all this weakness must be added the instability,
the lack of control, and the fragility already discussed; these
are facts. Her grasp on the world is thus more restricted;
she has less firmness and less steadiness available for projects
that in general she is less capable of carrying out. In other
words, her individual life is less rich than man's."

She doesn't deny the facts but she manages to deny the obvious
implications. The facts in themselves, she maintains, " . . . have
no significance. I deny that they establish for her a fixed and
inevitable destiny. They are insufficient for setting up a hierarchy of the sexes." (1)

She then goes on to state the classic social science position,
which no longer admits the existence of unchangeable entities
as determinants of characteristiçs such as those ascribed to women,
Jews, or Negroes. (These are badly chosen illustrations. The Jew
is a cultural phenomenon, female sex organs and black skin are
biological phenomena with cultural overlays. There is nothing
fixed about the Jew, but there *is* something fixed about the female
and the Negro.) She then goes on to make her version of the
familiar feminist charge, that men use their established position
to inculcate "inferiority complexes" in the female from infancy,
when she cannot resist. This complex persists throughout life
and comes to be regarded as "femininity."

Betty Friedan also acknowledges the power of early indoctrination, and gives the devil his due recognition as a Machiavellian
finagler. But she prefers to put the weight of her critique on
man's muscle power as the prime source of male dominion. Up
to the advent of the machine age, she says, survival required
muscle, which women didn't have and men did. Men dominated,
not only because they could enforce their will, but because they

had the critical survival gimmick. Now that muscle has given way to the machine and is therefore obsolete, men no longer have exclusive possession of the survival gimmick. Women can punch buttons as well as men. Therefore continued male domination is no longer legitimate, and continues only as a result of coercion. In Friedan's thinking,

$$machine = muscle = equality$$
or
$$machine = equality.$$

Now that muscle has been ciphered out of the equation, continued male domination is unethical, undemocratic, and outrageous.

If we ignore the patent weakness in this argument, that men can still use their muscle to knock women down and the machine can do nothing about it—which, while unethical, is not therefore unthinkable—there is still only a superficial plausibility to such reasoning. One sees no mad rush on the part of women to compete with truckdrivers, firefighters, garbage collectors, bricklayers, or combat infantrymen, even though their jobs have been mechanized. Nor is muscle without its irreplaceable uses, as any woman who has changed a flat tire on a hill in the hot sun can testify. Nor should we lightly dismiss a strength that might be very much in demand the next time the oceans rise forty feet, or an earthquake slides California into the Pacific, or some other catastrophe occurs. Muscle is millions of years old. Machinery has displaced it only during the last hundred years, for big jobs, and only during the last thirty years for small, domestic jobs. It is premature to write muscle off the books.

However, while this line of masculine rebuttal is sound enough, its weakness lies in the fact that it is essentially as trivial as what it rebuts—the argument that masculine muscle is the reason for female subordination. Muscle is not the reason for female subordination; at best it is only the instrument. Neither is cultural indoctrination.

Aggression is the reason for female subordination—an aggression which is given more to the male than to the female, in all mammals as well as in man.

The same phenomenon which is responsible for "territoriality" or population spacing in a species, and "hierarchy" or psychological status spacing in a society, is also responsible for the dominion of man over woman. And it is not likely to become obsolete.

Lack of insight into the fact that aggression, not muscle, makes the male supreme over the female, as well as lack of insight into the fact that equality implies equal responsibility as well as equal freedom, is what vitiates modern feminism.

It is because women fail completely to understand that male aggression is the source of male dominance, that we hear so much misdirected jazz about equality—a sound and a fury as irrelevant as it is tiresome. Democratic ideas are not commonly supposed to make one woman as pretty as another, nor one person as smart as another, but they are supposed to obliterate magically the real differences in aggressive endowment between the sexes. Fuzzy thinking in regard to just what is, and is not, democratic behavior, collaborates with ignorance as to the source of male domination, to deflect feminist attention away from the central and serious problem of modern woman, rather than toward it.

Of the 193 living species of ape, monkey, and man, only one, the spider monkey, sports a female sometimes bigger and stronger than the male, and none has any other form of social organization than a status hierarchy energized by aggression. The mammalian world is a world primarily organized around aggression. There is overwhelming evidence for this, if we will but stop and look at it.

One of the three neo-feminists I have chosen to debate, Ashley Montagu, is a living, if unwitting, demonstration of the fact that the male of the species is the major bearer of the aggressive endowment. Simone de Beauvoir merely acknowledges physical differences but denies that they justify inequality; Betty Friedan goes one step further in audacity and simply ignores the problem of physical differences; Ashley Montagu daringly takes the bull by the horns and goes to the other extreme. He makes a strength out of a weakness by taking the position that physical differences show women to be physically superior to men, and are thus doubly wronged by inequality! (2)

He takes the offensive by calling our attention to the fact that these "weak" creatures live longer than men, withstand stress better, score higher on intelligence tests, respond to certain stimuli faster, excel in rapid perception of detail, can shift attention more easily, etc., etc. He explains away their lesser accomplishments. These, he says, are due to their enforced sedentariness, which restricts their experience of the world as compared to that of the male. He also points out that practically every argument used to justify "inferior" races has been used to justify the "inferior" status for women, thereby implying that the position of women is what it is because of masculine prejudice.

Montagu also points out that while it is true that the male was built for effort, there is a price tag for the bigger body and greater power. Male expenditure of energy is greater and the man burns out more rapidly, as the mortality statistics show. All of this is true and not arguable. But without quite saying so directly, Montagu manages to hint that man is in a deadly parallel with the dinosaur, whose great size led to extinction, and he concludes that "in a society in which the strong destroy themselves, it is obviously not an advantage to be strong." War confers no survival benefits and is pathological. Neither does the domination of man over woman confer survival benefits. All of this is highly arguable, especially since the problem of war and the problem of male domination are forced into an association they do not really have.

The real reason, Montagu continues, why male domination persists is that men have a deep psychological need to hold women down. If women were allowed to compete with men as breadwinners, "man's claim to creativity" would be undermined. But men need this claim because deep down they are jealous of women's sacred ability to create life!

In this ingenious claim Montagu really evens up the score for women; for one of the most vexatious points classic Freudianism made against women was that they suffered from "penis envy," and were no more than second-rate men doomed forever to imitation. Now the position is reversed and it is man who is a second-rate woman!

To support his argument, Montagu cites *infibulation* and *subincision*. Infibulation is the barbaric practice, prevalent among North African primitives, of amputating the clitoris and labia at puberty and gang-raping the young girl, after which the vulva is sewn up, leaving just an opening to pass urine and menstrual fluids. When the girl is married, the opening is sufficiently enlarged to admit the spouse's penis, subsequently opened wider to permit childbirth, and then made smaller again! The motive for this savagery is obviously male jealousy of female procreative powers, which no one can deny. But that this is a pervasive characteristic of the male kind is disproved by the fact that the practice is limited to certain culture areas. The numbers of men involved are large, but that is because the cultures are themselves populous.

Subincision consists of the mutilation of the male. The underside of the young boy's penis is slit to imitate a crude vulva. The

word for the mutilated penis is the same as that for "vulva."
At periodic ceremonies the subincision is made to bleed, to imitate menstruation. Here, too, the motive is obviously jealousy of
female procreative powers; but the practice is open to the same
counter-argument: it is not universal.

Fortunately the understanding of our own kind has evolved to
the point that we do not have to view either women as second-
rate men, or men as second-rate women. Woman creates by pro-
creating, man creates by work. Each is programmed that way, as
science clearly demonstrates. Each is doing the thing that millions
of years have dictated. On the whole, men like being men and
women like being women. Even homosexual men for the most
part prefer being homosexual men to being women.

Now, although Ashley Montagu's line of argument can be
demolished at all points, he has at least faced squarely the issue
of biological difference which de Beauvoir skirts and Friedan
ignores, and he has done it by means of some original and creative thinking. But his efforts are unavailing. The dictum that
"anatomy is destiny" has by no means been laid to rest, as so
many social scientists think. It has merely not been brought up
to date. Recent developments have provided more than adequate
evidence for believing that men and women will never achieve
a state of perfect equality, even in the science-fiction future. And
though these developments should not be used to justify legal or
structural inequality, neither should we blind ourselves to the
obvious.

De Beauvoir, Friedan, and Montagu have some things in common besides feminism. What they take for granted and consider
beyond debate is as instructive to us as what they feel the need
to explicate. All three are either trained in the social sciences, or
strongly "social-science" in their orientation. This is obvious in
their writings, and it is one of the sources of the limitation of
their viewpoint. Certain kinds of evidence have no persuasive
power with them. That is, in the ancient debate about which
influence is decisive in the formation of the human personality—
innate drives or societal conditioning, heredity or environment—
the social scientist invariably opts for nurture over nature. If he
didn't he probably wouldn't be a social scientist. This bias is
natural for him, but the lay reader is frequently unaware of just
how "natural" that is.

In the first place, most social scientists, as I observed during
my years as a graduate student of sociology, have a distaste for
biology, and for the long hours of laboratory study it entails.

Insight, properly substantiated by a well designed field study, is the mode of work social scientists enjoy. They arrive at their conviction that the molding effects of culture are more decisive to personality formation than biological inheritance, through a study of culture alone. But cultural studies at this stage of the art are much too crude to permit biological factors to show through. This does not mean that biological factors are absent. The fact that swamp grass bends so easily to every passing breeze, does not mean that it lacks an inner structure. The structure itself bends with the wind, but it still shapes the blade. Sociological studies alone cannot declare on the presence or absence of biological drives. Sociology is too crude, and its point of view defines biology out. It will be for biologists looking for behavioral mechanisms to declare on that point. This leads to an associated point.

Crude as they may be, the social sciences are still the only guideposts we have had for the last hundred years. Though biology crystallized as a discipline much earlier, in one narrow area it never got off the ground. Biologically speaking, there was no effective study of human behavior during the decades when the social sciences were developing; social science, in all its resplendent crudity, preempted the field.

It was not until the 1930's that ethologists like Konrad Lorenz scored breakthroughs in the biological approach to behavior. And the luck of the game was such that the first pronouncements of ethology merely antagonized the social sciences. They sharpened the nature-nurture controversy by coming out in favor of innate aggression in man, which most sociologists and anthropologists vigorously deny.

Ashley Montagu has been among the most vociferous in condemnation of those ethologists who believe in innate aggression, for fear that such a belief would lead to a fatalistic acceptance of war and the brutality of man toward man. I submit that to stand against war and brutality is an important thing to do, and I fully support such a stance. But a political conviction is not an adequate reason for denying a scientific truth. The basic question is whether innate aggression exists or does not exist, not whether it will lead to war or not. Furthermore, the fear that such a proposition being believed might lead to a worsened condition for man, may be groundless. It may be that a knowledge of man's capacity for evil will shock people into being careful—more careful than a blind belief in the goodness of man has encouraged us to be. Possibly our exaggerated belief in the natural goodness of man, in which all man's evil is explained away as a result of bad environment, has caused more harm than the Puritanical belief that man is an inherent sinner. It certainly bears thinking about.

But a caveat must be entered here: Not all investigators on the learning side of the issue ignore biological factors, only those who study man. Those who study men in the flesh, the psychotherapists with a background in medicine and/or physiology, in large part accept innate factors, especially aggression. No one who has actually had to face the full force of the emotions of hate and hostility in patients can believe that these emotions have been induced by social factors alone. But so far the Erik Eriksons of this world have not been able to persuade the social scientists to recognize the constants recurring generation after generation, caused merely by being a child, an adolescent, an adult, and an aged person. Such a confrontation with individuals places limits on the concept of human plasticity. It is far easier to look at cultures and their standard types, and sweep the cultural deviant under the rug.

I have emphasized the vested interests of the social sciences because the problem is of some consequence to the study of masculinity and femininity. There are those who have reason to deny my central thesis—that male domination over the female is a function of the aggressive drive in man—on grounds other than the merits or demerits of the proposition. It affects their judgement. I am taking issue with the social-science-oriented, neo-feminist claim that all significant human behavior in the area of masculine-feminine personality formation, in the area of masculine-feminine identity, in the area of domination-subordination, and in the area of aggressiveness-passivity, is the result of cultural conditioning. Instead, I push the proposition that masculine-feminine patterns of behavior are biologically programmed before cultural influences get a chance to work. Cultural indoctrination merely picks up and continues the differentiated behavior genetically begun, and endocrinologically boosted. I am not talking about male-female *physical* differentiation. I am saying that masculine-feminine *behavior* starts at the biological level. Behavior is so closely linked to sex as to be inseparable from it. Specifically I am asserting that *men have been biologically programmed for domination, and women have been biologically programmed for subordination.* Boys on top and girls on the bottom is the biological directive for the emotional economy, as well as for sexual intercourse.

Having summed up the neo-feminist position and what I think

is generally wrong with it, and given my own broad conviction that male domination of the female is biologically determined and hence not subject to democratic dogma, it is time to outline my method of approach to the subject.

Insofar as the neo-feminist position is based on largely sociological considerations, it is necessarily a social-science type of approach; and insofar as my position is based mostly on the biological belief in innate aggression, my approach is necessarily a biological approach. However, the biological study of animal and human behavior—ethology—requires explanation; it is a relatively new way of looking at behavior and is still controversial.

Some critics of the ethological approach claim that it is engaged in circular reasoning and is hence invalid. They assert that ethologists project onto animal behavior subjective interpretations derived from introspection about their own private, human behavior. Ethologists then "discover" their own subjective input into the animals and label it "behavior." In short, they "humanize" animals and have no real proof of the validity of their interpretations.

Against this criticism there are two types of rebuttals. As for the first, much of our nonintellectual behavior stems from the cerebellum or old mammalian brain, and not from the cerebral cortex or new brain. Therefore, much human behavior stems from the same source as the behavior of other mammals. Simply watching the monkeys at the zoo masturbating confirms that.

But more importantly, there is solid objective support for the validity of the ethological approach: it can *control, condition,* and *modify* behavior, and *operationally produce new behavior* in the animals studied. Therefore, ethology must be doing something right. If operational success is the final criterion of valid performance in all other sciences, it should be good enough to justify the validity of the ethological way. Too many dogs, cats, and raccoons do the things we all do to justify the belief that humans stand on one side of a great divide, with all other creatures on the other, insofar as nonintellectual behavior is concerned.

But thinking is only one kind of behavior. There are others. The fact of the matter is that we are not only cut of the same cloth as the other higher mammals, but we actually get along better with dogs, cats, and raccoons than we do with our own kind. This is true of dogs, cats, and raccoons also. They are more hostile to their own kind than they are to humans.

This situation exists because there is aggression operating between dog and dog, cat and cat, raccoon and raccoon, and human and human, to space them out horizontally and vertically. But since dog and man, or cat and man, are not predator and prey, there is no aggression operating across the species. Aggression mostly operates between members of the same species.

Other humans, being aggressive, have power over us and can harm us, no matter how loving they are, so human love is always contaminated by an element of fear. But the love between human and pet is not inhibited by fear of aggression, and is therefore, in a manner of speaking, purer. It bears thinking about that we can often relate emotionally to a different species better than we can to members of our own. This is possible because aggression is absent.

But a qualification must be entered here. By asserting that male domination follows from the biological fact that males are more aggressive than females, I don't mean to imply that females are passive.

Both sexes are aggressive. A creature who is totally unaggressive simply could not survive, and my point is simply that the male is demonstrably *more* aggressive than the female.

The concept of female passivity has been as much of an irritant to the feminist as the idea of innate aggression has been a call to arms for the social scientist. While Montagu admits that the female is forced by circumstances to be more sedentary, he points out that this is an imposed characteristic rather than a biological one. If circumstances were different, he believes, the female would not be sedentary.

Nevertheless he must concede, along with de Beauvoir, that the male does have a five percent higher metabolic rate, a higher red blood cell count, and that he burns fuel faster than the female, which is a physiological way of saying that he is more vital than the female. He also goes beyond de Beauvoir and admits that behaviorally, the male infant is more active than the female. But to admit these physiological facts is to admit that the male is more aggressive than the female. These implications cannot be denied, but neither must they be overdrawn. Female passivity does not follow from physiological difference, though the lesser aggressiveness of the female does. Passivity and lesser aggressiveness are not synonymous concepts.

It may help to banish the myth of absolute female passivity if we regard the capacity for action as taking place along a gauged arc by which it can be measured. On the one end of the arc we have maximum activity—motion, aggressiveness, and aggression; on the other extreme we have minimum activity—little motion, negligible aggressiveness and aggression. Given the variability between individuals in both sexes, most males will be closer to the maximum end of the arc than females, although some females will place closer to the maximum end than some males.

In other words, the average or mean male of a given somatotype is more aggressive than his matching average or mean female of the same somatotype. It does not mean that the human female is a helpless, inert blob of protoplasm, incapable of initiative or decisive action, nor does it mean that all men are dynamic leaders.

Aggression and aggressiveness can obviously be amplified or subdued by social conditioning, but it is not a sole product of that conditioning. It is a biological endowment. The human male is part and parcel of the obvious trend in nature to build males bigger, stronger, tougher, and more pugnacious than females on a relative, but not on an absolute basis.

Other traits are inextricably linked with greater and lesser aggression. Toughness is invariably associated with greater aggressiveness and tenderness with lesser. The terms can be taken literally as well as figuratively. The skin of a man is tougher than woman's. So is his attitude. Both stem from the amount of aggression each is endowed with. The man, with more aggression, thrusts into the world more and experiences more abrasion, both physically and emotionally. The woman, with lesser aggression, interacts less with the outer world and experiences less wear and tear.

Yet toughness and tenderness are not mutually exclusive, any more than activity and passivity are. A man can be at the tough end of the scale when selling an insurance policy and at the tender end while bouncing his baby. But most of the time his life experiences call forth his toughness and hers call out her tenderness.

The combination of the fundamental error of not seeing that masculine domination follows from the edge man has in aggression, plus the second error of not seeing that masculinity and femininity are rooted in biology, and only secondarily in education, leads the feminists into making a third significant error. Believing the sexes to be fundamentally equal commodities differently packaged, the feminists treat them as equal when making comparisons, and make evaluations in terms of *superiority* and *inferiority*. They neglect to make a vital discrimination between two different ways in which females relate to males, and this failure to distinguish leads them to choose the wrong fork in the road of their development.

The terms superior and inferior are simply inadequate as a context for an understanding of the relations of the sexes. They obscure what should be illuminated. And the use of these terms also points to a generation gap between the neo-feminists and the neo-masculinists.

The new masculinist no more thinks of men as superior to women than he thinks of apples as superior to oranges. Male and female are both human. Apples and oranges are both fruits. No one would argue the superiority of one fruit over another, simply because they had a preference.

In like manner, no one should spend time fruitlessly arguing the superiority of one sex over the other. Each sex has its own thing to do, each individual is "equal" as a person before the law and before God. But in their actual face-to-face relationships men and women are not on a parity of power, no more so than is a child on a parity of power with an adult, a stupid man with an intelligent man, or a poor man with a rich man. This holds true even though the child, the stupid man, and the poor man are on a parity of right, according to our value system, with the adult, the intelligent man, and the rich man. Like parent and child, men and women are arranged in a "peck order" of power. In it, they are either dominant or subordinate to someone else.

For example, the sharecropper army sergeant may be dominant to the millionaire buck private, without anyone mistaking him as superior to the private. Likewise, the fact that women find themselves below men in the hierarchy of society does not make them inferior; it merely makes them subordinate.

But subordination is only one of the two ways in which women find themselves beneath men, and the concept of superiority obscures this important distinction. There are harmful consequences to understanding in the fact that the difference between subordination and dependence has been obliterated by the term superiority.

"Superior-inferior," "dominant-subordinate," and "independence-dependence" are similar terms and, in a rough sense, synonymous. But for our purposes they cannot be considered equivalent or interchangeable.

In the dialog of power between man and woman, domination-subordination must be defined as referring to rank in the peck order or hierarchy. The husband is dominant to the wife, who in turn is dominant to the child.

Independence-dependence refers to self-sufficiency. The wife is normally subordinate to the husband, but if she happens to be independently wealthy or holds a job, she is not dependent. If she has no money and holds no job then she is dependent as well as a subordinate. *All dependents are also necessarily subordinates, but not all subordinates are dependents.* The distinction will become clear as we use it, and it is absolutely crucial to an understanding of just how the sexes arrived at their present unbalanced relationship.

Superiority-inferiority usually have no meaning at all when applied across the sexes, unless we are comparing a strictly defined characteristic, like swimming ability, but they usually have more utility when comparing one member of a sex to another. John is superior to Jack at making money. Jane is superior to Jill in beauty. In general it only leads into a semantic swamp to make comparisons of superiority and inferiority between the sexes. It is in trying to get out of this bog that women were led in the wrong direction.

Thinking themselves inferior in status because of an unjust lack of equality, they have failed to see that they are *naturally* subordinate while only *accidentally* dependent, and thus they have sought redress by attacking that which was unchangeable instead of that which was accidental and alterable. Had they understood that they were not inferior, but simultaneously subordinate and dependent, they would have seen that it was not subordination that was crippling them, but dependence.

As I have pointed out, the two terms are analogous only in popular thought. In the same way, in the popular mind the terms "liberty," "equality," and "fraternity" all mean the same thing, though actually there are sharp distinctions between them.

Liberty and equality are no more synonymous than are subordination and dependence. In fact, they are in conflict. A lot of one implies a little of the other. One prospers at the expense of the other. One can have either equality or independence as a value, but not both simultaneously. When the neo-feminists once more sought equality as their grandmothers had done, without understanding that the lack of it was no longer a real problem, they necessarily turned away from the true solution to their problem, which lay along the path of independence, or liberty, or freedom, the latter terms being roughly synonymous.

In turning away from independence the neo-feminists also condemned themselves to remain blind to the importance of responsibility. Responsibility and independence are the opposite sides of the same coin, and one cannot legitimately have one without the other. The refusal to accept responsibility and the failure to reach for independence have kept women in a state of arrested development, unable to keep pace with change except through the reiteration of worn-out, obsolete responses.

There has been a significant chain of consequences to the failure of women to realize that it is greater male aggressiveness that puts women into a subordinate status, and that this is natural and unalterable (until such time as we displace nature as genetic comptroller). It has led them to seek equality where equality does not exist, and to fail to grasp the opportunity for growth, through independence, that lay within reach. Since the subordination of woman to man is *biological* whereas her dependence is *social,* the completion of her emancipation will be achieved not by altering her subordination, but by reducing her dependence to the absolute minimum necessary to fulfill her special biological function.

In redefining their objective, the feminists could profit from a study of the double-entry system of bookkeeping. In the money economy, matters are kept in balance by balancing debits against credits, or the entries on one side of the ledger will not equal the entries on the other side.

Feminists have not freed themselves from the intellectual error of balancing masculine credits against feminine debits, rather than balancing masculine credits against masculine debits and feminine credits against feminine debits. On the credit or plus side of the masculine ledger the man enjoys domination. On the debit or minus side he suffers responsibility. The woman's credits show little responsibility. Her debits show a balancing subordination entry. Some rigorous double-entry thinking by the feminists would eliminate the double standard they have unwittingly practised for years while accusing the men of the same.

Such sloppy thinking has led the neo-feminists to fail to apprise their young constituency of the real cost of "more" for women. That cost is the acceptance of greater responsibility. It should be fully realized and appreciated by the young women who are following the banner unfurled by their elder advisors.

The actual power relationship operant between the sexes cannot be adequately conveyed within the context of wishful or fuzzily democratic thinking, or self-serving social science. Many young women may find, when the issue is thoroughly explained to them, that they do not want to pay the cost, assuming they have a choice. On second thought, they may decide that they do not have as much in common with their feminist leaders as they do with men. Both Betty Friedan and Simone de Beauvoir write from the standpoint of women who are cramped the most—the able, assertive, highly-educated feminine intellectual. These women may be the most competent to announce where the shoe pinches but they may be the least qualified to prescribe the remedy, since they would presumably benefit most from the changes they propose. The rank and file might find themselves worse off than they were before. All women should be aware of the consequences, because all will bear them whether they are feminists or not.

In this chaotic world, there are indeed stresses and strains in the feminine role. But women are not suffering alone. There are also stresses and strains in the masculine role which, I intend to show, are much more painful, but are borne in silence.

Women are not yet sufficiently adept at distinguishing between frustrations which come their way because they are women, and those which come simply because they are also human beings. Everything painful that happens to a woman is not caused by her femaleness. The fact that she fails to be appointed president of the firm does not mean she has been unfairly discriminated against. She *was* discriminated against, but not necessarily unfairly. So were all the male candidates who lost—without excuses. Before the fair sex puts through another revolution it ought to be sure it has not called up a bulldozer to move an anthill.

It is my general contention that though the neo-feminists are correct in recognizing a deficiency in the feminine role, they have diagnosed it incorrectly and have misstated their case. They are putting forth fallacious arguments in defense of it. In rebuttal I would like to hazard the following propositions in defense of the masculine side:

(1) Men and women *are not* truly equal, except as persons before the law and before God.

(2) Men are *more* aggressive than women. They are genetically, glandularly, and psychologically programmed for dominance over women.

(3) Women are *less* aggressive than men. They are genetically, glandularly, and psychologically programmed for submission to men.

(4) *Masculine* and *feminine* roles are not created by society. They are initiated biologically, just as male and female are. Society merely elaborates what biology differentiated.

(5) Men need not be ashamed of their impulses towards mastery over women—though they must recognize responsible restrictions and limitations in that attempt.

(6) Women do not rate equality, except in the legal sense. But they do rate independence.

The above propositions are what I consider fact. The following propositions are not matters of fact, but statements of subjective personal opinion.

(A) Though the current neo-feminine agitation for equality is in error, it will continue—but for the wrong reasons. To be for feminine equality is now the same as being liberal. To be against it is the same as being reactionary.

(B) Therefore, life being so irrational, men must extract what tactical advantages they can from the situation. These happen to be enormous.

(C) Because—while women strive for an emancipation they cannot get, they will accidentally and unintentionally relieve men of the inequities of the man's role! None of this would have happened if women hadn't stirred the pot. In the parlance of the economists, *the price of women will fall.*

The real enemy of woman is not man and his strength and initiative, but her own weakness and lack of go. Which side one focuses on makes an enormous difference. If strength is the cause of the trouble, then male strength should be cut down to size, which means that the proper therapy for women is to make men weaker. But it is feminine weakness that is the problem, and it is this that needs eliminating or reducing. Therefore the proper strategy is not to weaken men but to make women stronger.

With varying degrees of emphasis, the feminists all believe that it is the relative difference in strength that accounts for man's dominance. But by some curious twist of logic they see man's strength as his failure and woman's weakness as her success. For them, it is not weakness which is regrettable, but strength. It is not woman who is held up to criticism for her failure to be strong; it is man who is criticized for his failure to be weak. It simply never occurs to them that woman's relative deprivation is her own fault, not man's. It is caused not by what man withholds from her, but by what she shirks doing for herself.

One would have to search far and wide to find a therapist who will accept the destruction of strength as a valid therapy, especially when the strength lies in an individual who is not a patient.

One does not cure a woman's cold by giving her husband an aspirin. The patient is woman. But she would cure herself by making the man sick.

We have arrived at the point where "proofs" are in order. In Part I, we shall deal with the possibilities of feminine equality. In Part II, we progress to the potentialities of feminine independence. In Part I, a body of facts is assembled; in Part II, it is put to work.

PART I
THE AWFUL TRUTH ABOUT FEMININE EQUALITY

Aggression and
Feminine Subordination

If male aggression is really the reason for feminine subordination, how has it been obscured for so long? Why have male muscle, sedentary living, and inferiority complexes been offered as sufficient causes for male domination? After all, Freud recognized the existence of human aggression three generations ago, and thinkers have been aware of human savagery for several thousand years. Why was not the basic link between feminine inequality and male aggression discovered long before this?

It is because both the strength and the weakness of psychoanalysis lies in the fact that it confronts single individuals, and the group only indirectly by inference, or not at all. Because analysts looked only at one individual at a time, they could not see the social function of aggression. To perceive it, one must look at groups. As long as one perceives aggression in isolated individuals only, it looks like a useless remnant from a primordial past. One cannot see what positive need it fills, what constructive work it does. Not seeing the whole truth about aggression, the analysts were unaware of how much behavior it explained.

It remained for ethologists, studying nonhuman groups, to discover what aggression was all about. They were the first to recognize it as the fundamental organizing principle of social groups, the first to see that, by exercising aggression, members of a species were prevented from getting more populous than a given area could support. Aggression spaces out members of a species, and while evolving to space out solitary animals, it also made social living possible through psychological spacing into peck orders.

Far from being a leftover from a primordial past, like the useless appendix, aggression is as important to the species as the unconscious is to the psyche of the individual, or mutation to evolution, or gravity to celestial mechanics. The discovery that aggression spaces, was an epochal one. When sociology incorporates this concept, it will for the first time have a firm principle that does not evaporate under changing cultural conditions. By means of it, the social sciences can begin to move out of the Stone Age into the 20th century.

Another reason why the importance of aggression went unrecognized for so long is that the most overt manifestations—the aggression of predator toward prey—was seen as the whole, whereas it is in fact only a part of aggression. This kind of aggression is spectacular, but it is not as primary as spacing aggression, which existed before predatory aggression. Predatory aggression evolves out of spacing aggression, not spacing aggression out of predatory aggression. Creatures were aggressive before predatory behavior evolved, but the sheer drama of predatory aggression paralyzed true observation. Nature was not as red in tooth and claw as had always been thought. Most creatures in nature lived side by side peacefully; the tooth and claw business applied only to those who stood in the relationship of prey and predator.

Also, much of the fighting that men observed was incorrectly attributed to predation, and was actually only the ritual combat of the spacing mechanism. Two bucks locking horns over a female in estrus might have looked like mortal struggle, but actually it was not. Usually, though not always, it terminated without bloodshed. The weaker animal usually broke off combat by fleeing, and spacing was accomplished. Most of the fighting in nature is of this type. Only a few creatures fight to the death over females or territory.

It was not until the significance of spacing aggression became clear for the lower orders, that its meaning for human social life became manifest. That is a very recent discovery. Not all forms of aggression have yet been traced to the behavior it is responsible for; that is why the domination of the human male over the human female has not yet been explained by aggression. Sooner or later the connection would have been made. But the so-called "lower" orders knew it before we did. The baboon, for example, clearly understands the differences in aggression of the human male and female. In South Africa, raiding baboons will not run away from a farmer's wife, though they take to their heels when the farmer himself appears!

In fact, the human female is exposed to two independent types of aggression from her male, each in itself sufficient to subordinate her. Together they clinch the job. Spacing aggression is only the lesser cause of feminine subordination; the first and more powerful cause is sexual aggression.

Both these forms of aggression are obviously "innate," in spite of the fact that so many people hate that word. In all species, aggression appeared millions of years before intelligence; therefore, as most species have very little learning capacity, most of their behavior must be "innate." This also holds true for the mental genius, man. It is clear in our own case that we became predators long before we became intelligent; therefore, the aggressive aspects of our behavior must also be innate rather than learned.

No one would really care one way or another, if it were not for the fact that man is obviously the biggest killer of them all. Our innate aggression implies to many that war is inevitable, and this is a conclusion they cannot abide. Not believing that war is inevitable, they will not believe that aggression is innate. Thus, as they think the masculine penchant for making war is intimately linked to the masculine penchant for dominating women, they also find themselves against masculine domination and support the feminist demand for equality.

But this association is a misalliance. Warfare among humans stems from spacing aggression and predatory aggression. Feminine subordination stems from spacing aggression and sexual aggression. If spacing aggression were to dry up overnight, the human female would still be exposed to sexual aggression, which is more powerful than spacing aggression. Therefore there is no reason why a masculinist should come into conflict with antiwar principles. An individual can be antiwar and promasculine.

There is another reason why the antiwar people need not reject the innateness of aggression: It is very possible that human spacing and predatory aggression is subject to neurochemical control. In rats the killing mechanism is located in the hypothalamus, and can be suppressed or neutralized by chemical means. If this is true for rats, it is quite possibly true for humans, as the physiology of mice and rats seems to be close enough to that of humans to make them our primary victims of experimentation. The future looks quite bright for abolishing war.

Ashley Montagu argues against the innateness of aggression by linking it to the death instinct. He then points out that most psychoanalysts now repudiate Freud's notion of a death instinct, and thereby implies that innate aggression has also been repudiated. But the repudiation of the death instinct does not imply the sympathetic death of innate aggression; mounting evidence continues to indicate that aggression is as innate as a drive can be. I will shortly show that the ethological evidence for feminine subordination by reason of aggression is firmly supported by genetic, endocrinological, and psychological evidence. If that doesn't make aggression innate and feminine subordination natural, I don't know what *innate* and *natural* mean.

It will help the novice to understand aggression better if we elaborate on it for a moment. To define aggression precisely is impossible, so I must be content to use it as a loosely defined term. At the bottom of every system of thought there are such loosely defined terms. Usually they are the most important, the least important ones being amenable to the most precise definition. This indicates an unfortunate limitation of human intelligence, but we must live with it. Attempts at definition do at least have the merit of deepening our sense of the meaning. We may not arrive at precise understanding but we know more than we did before.

Earlier, when talking about aggression and passivity, I used passivity as a synonym for "stillness" or "inertness," thus presenting aggression as "motion" or "activity." This is almost, but not quite, true. All things that are alive are in motion and aggressive. Freud called this simple aliveness and motion the *Id*. But aggression differs from simple aliveness in that it is a directed thrust into the environment, of which initiative is an important aspect. Any organism that hunts for food is being aggressive—not merely the lion stalking his prey but also the cow searching for grass. In any organism the absence of motion is death, its presence is life. But aggression is more than the *Ego* shaping itself to mediate between the Id and outer reality. It is life taking the initiative, thrusting out for its own growth and survival. Some of this thrust is directed towards a source of life-supporting energy, and part of it is directed against forces that can deny the source of energy. Thus, in solitary animals, territorial aggression spaces individuals out so that each has a sufficient supply of energy. Status spacing aggression in social animals is another way of distributing the limited energy or fuel supply, providing more to those who need more sustenance and are more important to the society (the leaders), and less to those who need less, and are less important to the group's survival (the smaller, weaker animals). Sexual aggression provides for the continuance of the species by insuring that the sperm gets to the egg and fertilizes it. (It also provides that the egg be fertilized by a sperm of the type of animal most capable of surviving—the dominants.) Predatory aggression is simply a specialized form of aggression for an animal which has specialized in one form of diet—meat.

Whereas territorial and status spacing aggression provide for the individual, sexual aggression provides for the species, and is, in fact, a debit against the individual, because it lessens individual survival capacity. The need to bear young exposes the female to greater burdens and danger. The need to protect the young exposes the male to more danger than he would normally be exposed to, because fleeing is denied him as a way of escape.

The waiting egg is in a protected area, as it must be, and the sperm must find and penetrate this area. Thus, on the simple physical level, sexual aggression is the insertion and ejaculation of the penis in the vagina. But on the psychological level, aggression is the hunting out of the female, her wooing, or her raping, if she presents obstacles.

The basic aggression of the male in seeking out and wooing or forcing the female to copulate, defines the male posture towards the female. It is not a rigidly compartmentalized behavior, but is generalized at all levels. *The dominion of the male over the female has its origin in the sex act. It is the prime source of inequality between the sexes and will continue to be so long as humans copulate.* In addition to this force subordinating females, there is the downward thrust of intraspecific aggression, pushing the female to lower ranks in the group.

Territoriality is not always a matter of protecting a sufficient food supply for an individual. Sometimes it just means *Lebensraum;* some species will space themselves out in the conventional manner and then get food outside their territory.

But whether they eat at home or out, they space themselves out by threat displays and ritual fighting. If one animal has possession of a certain piece of turf and another tries to claim it, the occupant usually threatens to fight and the intruder withdraws. It is more economical of the intruder's time and energy to find an empty space than to fight for an occupied one. On the other hand, it is more economical for the occupant to fight than to be constantly dispossessed by intruders. Bravery is usually allocated to the occupant and cowardice to the intruder. When the occupant, at another time, stumbles into the territory of the former intruder, he then displays cowardice and runs away and the former intruder shows courage.

In cases where a fight actually takes place it is usually a threat display, in which each tries to look big, tough, and unbeatable. Once they tangle and find out which is stronger and which weaker, the weaker runs away or makes submissive gestures. The victor is appeased and quits with his symbolic victory. Hierarchies are created in the same manner.

Through threat, ritual fighting, and submissive gestures or flight, spacing aggression is kept under control. This method rarely leads to injury or death, and when it does it is by accident. Yet, from the human standpoint, it is the most vicious kind of aggression, because it liberates the emotions of hatred and hostility, and attaches pleasure to them. It is the kind of aggression that causes murder and war in human society, where controls are lacking.

A dramatic example of how much pleasure this kind of aggression gives to man was given in the controversial film, *The Wild Bunch*. A gang of American outlaws working for an army of guerillas in Mexico, suffers one of their members to be tortured by the guerilla general. Superior numbers cow them. But when the general finishes off their friend by cutting his throat, the Americans respond by killing the general. Having done so, they are stunned. So is the guerilla army. At this moment of disorganization, the Americans had their chance to escape. But the reckless killing of the general has whetted their blood lust. Instead of making good their escape, they start killing off the general's assistants, as though they were in a shooting gallery, taking obvious satisfaction as their guns explode and the bodies drop. They do this even though aware that they have lost their chance at escape and will be overcome by superior numbers. They choose to risk death in an orgy of killing, and they die in the knowledge that they have killed dozens of their enemies.

This kind of pleasure in killing is conspicuously absent in the aggression of a predator. Closing in on his prey does not release emotions of hatred, hostility, and viciousness. Neither does the predator take pleasure in what he is doing. Such emotions contribute nothing to his efficiency; they would, in fact, cause him to lose his cool and cramp his style. The cat tormenting a mouse does not hate it, nor does it take pleasure in eventually killing it, though the cat does take pleasure in its own technique. But this is a minor satisfaction, induced not by the kill but by the exercising of its skill. The same goes for a lion bringing down an antelope. It does not hate the antelope, and does not kill it for sport; only men do that. The lion kills in order to feed. As it can be seen to express disappointment when it misses, it must also feel some satisfaction when it succeeds, but only because it succeeded. Predatory aggression does not give pleasure. Only spacing aggression in man confers pleasure with the process of killing itself.

But how is it possible that aggression whose purpose is killing, does not lead to war, while aggression whose purpose is only spacing, not killing, *does* lead to war and murder, in humans? The answer lies in the fact that predatory aggression is important only to the survival of the individual animal, whereas spacing aggression is important for the survival of the whole species.

The powerful emotions of hate, fear, and pleasure which are attached to spacing aggression, are in themselves an indication of how important it was to get the individuals of a species spaced properly. Spacing aggression is the most important social mechanism at work among social animals. Without it, society could not exist.

But the critical point is that when the objective is achieved, when the loser flees, the aggression terminates. In species with built-in weaponry such as tooth and claw, fighting must cease upon the defeat of the weaker, because the drive is so powerful that it would otherwise wipe out the species.

Only for the one creature that lacks built-in weapons, man, does spacing aggression lead to death. During most of the history of man, fighting has not ceased upon the submission or defeat of the weaker. The weaker combatant is not allowed to submit but is either killed outright, or tortured to death. Man has not had time to perfect a method of control over his own spacing mechanism. Evolution is not all behind us—some lies still ahead. Appeasement gestures from the vanquished do not turn off our blood lust.

This inability of man to stop fighting when one combatant submits, is related to the fact that his weapons are artificial rather than natural. Other species, equipped with claws and teeth, must fight face to face and close up. They can see when one or the other is defeated. Man's weapons, after the sword, pushed him away from his enemy, so that he could not see the enemy's submission or appeasement gestures. Even when he could, he could not always turn off his desire to kill. The "prisoner of war" gimmick is a very modern invention. It was not always scrupulously observed by either side even as recently as World War II. Anyone in doubt need only ask a marine veteran of the Pacific campaign how many surrendered Japanese lived to get into a prisoner stockade. But perhaps we should be thankful for what progress we have made. Killing strangers outside our tribe is still *de rigueur* in time of war. But killing people inside the tribe is forbidden at all times, and severely punished as murder.

Until recently, evidence for the fact that man has aggravated the lack of control mechanisms over fighting by inventing weapons that work at a distance, was only of the subjective type that critics of ethology deplore. But now we have experimental verification, from the type of study that social scientists prize. As an example of the subjective kind of evidence, I offer first my own wartime experience as a navigator-bombardier.

I found no difficulty whatsoever in dropping bombs through a cloud cover at a point on a radar screen, from a height of five miles. It was much more difficult to pull the trigger on attacking planes. At one unforgettable moment, when a crippled German fighter plane drifted helplessly across my line of fire and I could have riddled it without lifting my .50 caliber from its sling, I didn't pull the trigger. I was about to, when the plane drifted close enough for me to see the pilot's face—the first and only time I ever saw an enemy during the war. His face was drained of blood and his head was snapping from side to side, desperately looking for a way out of the wall of fire he was drifting into. I could not administer the coup de grace and he drifted past, out of range. A few seconds later he blew up, so my defection from duty didn't matter. But I can still remember the shock of realizing that there was *a man* in that machine, dying like a trapped animal. Yet after that mission I continued to drop many more bomb loads on cities of no military value, without the slightest hesitation.

But since this type of evidence is rejected by social scientists as too subjective, its experimental verification in the laboratory is important. In a recent study, designed to find out how many of us are Eichmanns capable of committing any atrocity on orders from superiors, Professor Stanley Milgram found out not only that most of us are indeed Eichmanns, and will commit any atrocity on orders from our respected superiors, but that we do it the more willingly the farther away we are from the victim.

As long as the victim was out of sight in another room, 66% of the subject-Eichmanns delivered an electric shock to a victim of an intensity they had reason to believe was dangerous as well as punishing. When they could hear the victim protest, the rate fell off to 62.5%. When the victim was brought into the same room as the subject, the rate fell to 40%. When the subject actually had to touch the victim while administering the shock, the rate dropped to 30%. The closer the subject-aggressor came to the victim, the less willing he was to hurt him. Others may dispute the significance of this experiment, but until a better one is designed I will accept it as evidence that the spear is more dangerous than the sword.

However, the fact remains that even when men can see the defeat of their enemy, they still frequently can't stop killing them. The reason must be that man takes more pleasure in killing than other creatures, and is more predatory. And that is due to the fact that he entered the competition late, after most other predators were established and efficiently designed for predation by the evolutionary process. It is man's inferiority as a predator that accounts for his excesses in aggression. Unendowed with natural weapons, he was forced to invent them, and this invention became one of the critical factors that distinguished him from the other anthropoids.

Surprisingly enough, a memory trace of this differentiation is contained in the Adam and Eve fable, which turns out to be less fabulous than other ancient tales.

Our simian ancestor was a peaceful herbivore, living in trees and subsisting on fruit. He lived in a Garden of Eden without toil, and had only to stretch out his arm to obtain delicious food. A tree and its fruit were central facts in his life.

About 14,000,000 years ago, a crisis disturbed the easygoing life of this tree dweller. Climactic change on a global scale began to contract the vast forests that covered most of Europe and Asia. These were replaced by open steppe or plain. As this change progressed, the fruit supply dwindled too, and our ancestral Adam was forced to compete and struggle for food that had formerly been there for the taking.

He was faced with a crucial choice: He could either stay with the shrinking forest and fight for his share of less food, or he could abandon the forest and go down to the plain to seek new sources of food there. To stay in the trees meant to compete with his own kind. To descend to the plain meant to compete with animals already well adapted to it. Either way signaled the end of leisure and the beginning of work. Some of these prehistoric Adams elected to stay in the trees. They were the ancestors of the creatures we today pen up in the zoo.

Others left the forest—expelled by a food shortage—and started grubbing in the dirt for roots and bulbs, which was "work by the sweat of the brow." Thus was Adam pushed out of his Eden into a life of toil.

This Adam was a sorry spectacle indeed. He was not only a formerly leisured lord reduced to menial labor, he was an incompetent laborer as well. To supplement his grubbings he even increased his intake of ants and mice, a habit left over from his lemur past. They were good sources of protein but also graphic testimony to his poor foraging.

In time, he graduated to a better source of vital protein: He learned to scavenge on the carcasses of larger animals brought down by meat-eating predators. Now he became definitely carnivorous as well as herbivorous, which was a giant step forward.

But he was still a lowly creature, ill-adapted, and living off the leavings of more efficient creatures. Though the ground was fantastically rich in protein in the form of meat, he could not get at these riches directly for lack of tooth and claw.

But there came a day when he found a way, and changed from passive scavenger to active hunter. By hunting in groups he made up for his muscular weakness; and by inventing weapons he got his claws and teeth. He became not simply a predator, but a social predator. Of the 193 surviving anthropoids he was the first to make the transition to predation, closely followed by the baboon.

This effort to adapt cost him much. He had to develop a great deal of aggression to compensate for his basic inefficiency in this environment. And he has not been at it long enough to develop appropriate inhibiting mechanisms (which were already built into other species) against killing his own kind. Thus he won short-term survival at the expense of long-term survival.

As long as his weapons were crude, he was not in danger of extinction. But the moment they became sophisticated he was thrust back into crisis. Now, without innate inhibitions to control his drives, with killing power in excess, and with a penchant for attacking his own kind, he was right back where he had been 14,000,000 years earlier when the forests receded.

Hints of the coming crisis came immediately after his discovery of agriculture led to a population expansion. The earliest civilizations in the Nile and Euphrates valleys, given leisure by agricultural surpluses, used their spare time to start killing each other off on a grand scale.

Man's spacing mechanism had been set for small tribes and hunting parties—say five to fifty individuals. In the cities it broke down completely. The crowding stimulated the aggression which should have been relieved by spacing, but the spacing didn't take place and the aggression wasn't relieved. We now have experimental evidence that overcrowding which cannot be relieved results in social breakdown. In rats, population saturation produces psychosis and murder. But the ancients didn't know that there was an upper limit to safety in population density and their civilizations destroyed themselves. We moderns found out about it only after populations had soared past their former numbers.

The fact that excessive population is pressuring our spacing mechanism into working overtime, does nothing to decrease the intensity of the drive to subordinate the female. Even under normal conditions, spacing aggression works to subordinate her, adding its force to that of sexual aggression. In an overpopulated world, it exerts even more pressure in that direction.

Now, while the human species is a predatory species, heavily endowed with aggression, the two sexes do not share equally in this inheritance. The load of genetic aggression delivered to men is much larger than that delivered to women. It was man who evolved as a hunter, not woman. Even as Adam in the Garden of Eden, man was not without his ration of aggression, though his lazy way of life cannot have triggered it often. In most, if not all, of the prehuman types, he had been sexually dominant, and had pushed and shoved a little for status. But when he made a commitment to predation he became, relative to the female, a specialist in aggression. And his increase in predatory aggression seems to have increased his spacing and sexual aggression as well.

Exactly how this happened is not yet clear, but the process can be traced in general outline. Of the various types of early hominids that have been classified, one, the australopithecine, sported a female of the same body size as the male, and with equally developed canine teeth. This suggests that at that point in time both the male and female of the species lived without dominance, and both hunted.

If this type should turn out to be in the main line of our evolution, the female clearly lost her canine teeth and equal stature at some later time, and became a nonhunter. On the other hand, if it should turn out to be merely a collateral line of descent then it is likely that the female simply never passed through that phase of evolution.

All available evidence indicates that, unlike other predator species, the human female did not hunt or practice war. While her pregnancies are longer than that of any other species, this alone would not have kept her from the hunt. (Among some primitives, a woman is back on the job within an hour after childbirth. On the trail, she will drop out, have the child, and catch up with the main party at the next rest stop.) It was the prolonged dependency of the human child that made her unavailable for hunting; and, of course, her polarization about tenderness made hunting unattractive to her.

Not only does gross anatomy indicate that the human female did not pass through an evolutionary sequence as a hunter. Close inspection reveals three further decisive bits of evidence.

To begin with, her wide pelvis gives her a shorter step—per equal length of leg—than the male's. That is, for the same somatotype, the female leg will neither swing back and forth as fast, nor take as wide a step, as the male leg. Obviously this anatomical difference could never have developed if the woman had been doing what the man had been doing.

Secondly, the female cannot discharge her body heat as well as the male, and this ability is absolutely crucial to involvement in combat or crisis. It is, in fact, so important that the human type had to lose its covering of body hair in order to expedite its acquisition. This difference alone would support the argument that women did not wage war or hunt.

Thirdly, the human female cannot throw a spear as well as a male, and therefore was not as good at killing game. The human female's throwing style is closer to that of a chimpanzee or gorilla than it is to that of the human male. Man's throwing style, whether of a baseball or a spear, is absolutely unique among primates. The fact that the female cannot duplicate it, indicates that in this respect also, she failed to cross the threshold into hunting as the male did. It also indicates that she never developed the same kind of aggression.

If this array of physiological and anatomical evidence does not suffice to convince the skeptic, we can extend it to its social consequences: If man is physiologically a hunting beast and woman is not, we should be able to see the consequences in society and behavior. We can.

In virtually all cultures where hunting is important as a source of food men always handle weaponry, hunting, and war (as well as metalworking and hard labor). Women always handle cooking and gathering.

In almost all cultures boys are trained to be aggressive and girls are trained not to be. Margaret Mead points out that ownership of weapons—as distinct from tools—is usually restricted to males. Certainly this pervasive cultural style could not have developed if our women had hunted or waged war.

Such examples as we have of warring women are mostly drawn from "civilized" societies in the contemporary world drugged on war. In World War II, Russian women fought as guerillas. Indonesian women have done the same. Israeli women currently fight as combat troops. But among "primitives" such conduct is considered primitive.

Among mammals, ritualized fighting is exclusively a male affair. The females watch, and sometimes go with the winner. Females *will* fight—in defense of their young or in self-defense, or for scarce food, or for a male. But they rarely start a fight.

These ethological and anthropological observations are overwhelmingly supported by genetic, glandular, and psychological evidence. The female is on the short end of the aggressive endowment.

Since we have been predators for about 10,000,000 years, there is little reason to think that our aggression is not as innate as that of other species. It was developed long before our cerebral cortex, so we were predators long before we were smart. If aggression came before learning ability it must have been innate, and so, in consequence, is the male domination that flows from it, however unpalatable that may be to neo-feminists. But it need be no great tragedy that shatters our democratic values.

Unlike sexuality, aggression is not expressed without stimulus. If it is not triggered, it is merely potential energy that never becomes kinetic. Therein lies the secret of control over it. However, if a wet diaper on a baby is sufficient to trigger the baby's aggression, it is not likely that we can wipe out aggression entirely short of chemical means. Though military-industrial complexes, state departments, and politicians can be dismantled and neutralized, and war abolished, people are still likely to continue hurling insults and fists at one another. This will be irksome, but not fatal.

It is not the killing aggression of predator for prey that threatens the survival of humanity; we have channeled that into the slaughterhouse. What is left, is taken out on the deer during hunting season. It is the spacing aggression, releasing emotions of hatred unchecked by inhibiting mechanisms, that leads to murder and genocide on an epic scale. This is the type of aggression which rightly concerns our scientists now, and they have had little time to spend on the lesser problem of sexual aggression as the source of the dominion of the human male over the female. But this source of aggression is more powerful in humans than in other species, because humans are much sexier.

It is obvious that the human female does not have the aggression of the hunting females of other predator species, like the wolf or lion. She is significantly less aggressive than her spouse in her own species. And being sexier, with a longer gestation period, and years of caring for helpless children, she is definitely more tender and maternal than the females of other species. That this maternal tenderness is not culturally produced is shown by the amount of motherly devotion observable in the monkey and baboon, our near relatives. The human female has little chance of winning equality of power with the male, being so much less combative than he.

The female of our kind was already a subordinate creature when she accompanied Adam down from the trees. She became even more subordinate when Adam became a predator and she did not. Losing out in the aggression department, she slid over the border into dependency. Among other simian species, it is the female rather than the male who provides food for her young. She may cadge choice morsels for herself from the male, but basically she is her own food scrounger. Thus, while subordinate, the simian female is not dependent. This factor is vitally important to an understanding of the history of the human female.

While the male was evolving towards more and more aggressiveness and toughness, the female was not simply standing still. She was evolving in the direction of being more comfortable in the subordinate role. As she became more tender, she learned to find her deepest pleasure, reward, and satisfaction in subordination. Men did not simply dominate her; she actively subordinated herself to them. At every level of organization—genetic, glandular, psychological, and intellectual—male and female complement each other. There can be no mistaking the message. Nature has made a commitment to male dominance—though she will allow that commitment to be overridden to permit adaptation to continue, to keep the evolutionary options open. A radical change in the circumstances of man could reverse this commitment, and contemporary technological development *may be* such a radical change. I doubt it, though the neo-feminists do not. The present organization of society about its means of production, is in the long run, untenable. As it is bound to change, the ground under the claim to equality will crumble away.

The ethological evidence for the profound differences between male and female aggressiveness no longer stands alone. It is supported by the hard evidence of genetics and endocrinology; and certain basic, psychological facts, far from new, at last fall into place in the aggression scheme.

The Message
From the Genes

Maleness and femaleness, like every other characteristic of life, is determined by genes. In humans, each body cell contains about 40,000 of them. To combine, recombine, and generally utilize 40,000 genes per cell is a formidable engineering task, necessitating the evolution of a device of grouping genes into sets, or patterns, of chromosomes. These chromosomes are then manipulated as a whole instead of each and every gene separately.

A chromosome, or set of genes, is a long rodlike structure along which the individual genes are distributed in ordered arrangements. Every gene must be in a certain predetermined position on the surface of the chromosome in order to function in its appointed way. If it is out of its proper position, it will function differently from the way it should, or perhaps not function at all. Worse yet, it may produce a deformed offspring, or a dead one.

In a normal plant or animal, there is a fixed and unvarying number of chromosomes which determines the species characteristics. In humans, the magic number of chromosomes is forty-six. (Chimpanzees, gorillas, and orangutans have forty-eight.) Two of these forty-six chromosomes determine male or female sexuality. One of these two, the X chromosome, comes from the female parent; the other, an X or a Y chromosome, comes from the male parent. A new human being is created by the joining of these two chromosomes into a pair. The other forty-four autosomes determine all other characteristics of the infant, but they also contain some genes that make a little contribution towards sexual type. How these two sex chromosomes combine, or fail to combine, determines not only maleness and femaleness, but whether the fetus will be healthy or deformed.

The X- or female-determining chromosome is the longer one by far, enabling it to carry a far richer load of genes on its surface than the male one. The male chromosome, with its smaller load-carrying surface, does not even use all of that; much of its surface is devoid of genes. More importantly, some of the few genes there are on the Y chromosome, have no matches on the female chromosome. This means that the male has some sex-related characteristics which the female lacks. It is possible that one or more of these unmatched genes is responsible for aggression. I read the evidence to point that way.

According to geneticists, the female chromosome seems to be very stable and to have undergone little evolutionary change. The male chromosome, on the other hand, is not only shorter but appears to have been subjected to more evolutionary wear and tear. In fact, most of the mutations that occur seem to happen to the male chromosome, rather than being equally distributed between the sexes. Thus, what is happening on the genetic level seems to confirm, roughly, what we see on the higher level of human behavior: Women appear to be more conservative and life-preserving. Men appear to be more adventurous and life-risking. Each behavior pattern is biologically adaptive and in accord with what we would expect. Nature gambles with the male and plays it safe with the female.

Feminists such as Montagu have crowed at the "healthier" appearance of the female chromosome, maintaining that its larger size indicates greater robustness. But this notion has no more validity than the argument of the older masculinists—that where it counts, the male chromosome is decisive and overrides the female chromosome. It is true that one Y will produce a male offspring, even under aberrant circumstances where it is teamed up with two X's, rather than the normal one. But it could hardly do anything else.

Neither the larger size of the female chromosome nor the overriding quality of the male one is significant. Each does its intended job.

The egg of the parent female always and unvaryingly carries X chromosomes in its cells. The male sperm carries half a cargo of X and half a cargo of Y chromosomes. Thus, all of the parent female's effort goes into creating another female, while half of the male parent's effort goes into creating a male, and the other half goes into making a female. When an X-bearing sperm fertilizes an X egg, an XX female is created. When a Y-bearing sperm fertilizes an X egg, an XY male is created. Or, an X chromosome from each parent begets a female child, an X from the mother and a Y from the father creates a male child.

About four out of the 40,000 genes a child inherits will be defective, statistically speaking. Against defects of the female chromosome, the female child has a marvellous defense, whereas the male has none. As the female is the result of a combination of two X's, all her genes will come in identical pairs. Her defective gene will be matched by a normal one on the other chromosome. The genes act in such a way that the normal gene will override, or support, or shore up, or function for, the defective one, and the female fetus will be normal.

But when the fetus is a male, the genes will not be in matching pairs, and there will be no corresponding gene on the Y chromosome to shore up the operation of a defective gene on the X chromosome. The defective gene from the female chromosome will express itself in the male offspring. The male fetus will either be killed off, or be deformed or deficient in some way. Thus, in a sense, the sins of the female chromosome are visited on the male offspring much more than on the female—because of the laws of arithmetic combination, not because the male chromosome is inferior. The male is truly nature's sacrificial creature. He is expendable on the genetic, as well as on the organic, level.

The fact that one normal gene will override its abnormal mate, plus the fact that the female egg can only make a female, while the male sperm can make either male or female, means that tissue is not basically neuter, but is prejudiced in favor of the female. Its normal thrust is to become female.

In cases where chromosomes fail to pair properly, a single female chromosome can create a fetus that will survive, albeit defectively. On the other hand, a fetus accidentally sired by one male Y chromosome, without an X partner, will not survive at all—except under the highly artificial circumstances of the laboratory. The male fetus must be able to draw upon the instructions of a female X chromosome as well as of a male Y, or he cannot make it, because it is the female X chromosome that is carrying the bulk of the genes. Without the female X most of the instructions for building are missing, and the process of fetus construction cannot take place. Tissue is basically female, not male, unless overridden by a male sex determinant. In some lower forms of life, and in the laboratory for higher forms, an egg can be fertilized without sperm, and grow to healthy adulthood. Eggs, then, are the true reproductive agents, not sperm. The function of the sperm seems to be limited to *irritating* an egg into development, and creating an offspring which is a specialist in aggression.

This genetic prejudice in favor of the female places severe strains on the male. One of the most significant of these is that a hereditary defect on the Y chromosome of the father can be passed on to the son only, not to the daughter, and is likely to express itself, whereas a defect in the mother's X chromosome, although it can be passed on to either son or daughter, is likely to be recessive and not express itself. This means in effect that genetic defects are likely to show up much more frequently in the male than in the female, even when the defect originates on the female chromosome. Consider, for example, the case of hemophilia, or bleeder's disease, which is caused by a defective gene on the female chromosome.

Hemophilia is usually lethal. Frequently the embryo dies in the uterus. When a daughter receives a hemophilia-defective gene on one of her two X chromosomes, she usually has a healthy one on the chromosome she inherited from her other parent, which shores it up. Therefore, the defective gene fails to act in her. It is recessive, and she will survive to pass it on to her male offspring, except in the unlikely event that she inherits two such defects at the same time, which would be statistically extraordinary.

But when the son receives this gene from his mother there is no matching gene on his Y chromosome to shore it up. Therefore the defect is malignantly expressed in him, and if he doesn't die before birth he will usually die before reaching the age of reproduction, and will not pass the defect on.

For hemophilia, there are fifty-seven male deaths per 100,000 population, and only two female deaths per 100,000 population, though it is a defect of the female chromosome. In like manner, color blindness, which is also a female chromosomal defect, afflicts 8% of American males, but only 0.5% of females.

In *The Natural Superiority of Women* Ashley Montagu lists more than thirty serious defects of the female chromosome that show up predominantly in the male, and uses this list as an argument in favor of the superiority of women. His list is verified by other sources. Among female chromosomal defects that afflict the male are: albinism of the eyes, middle ear disease, gamma globulin deficiency, shortage of tooth enamel, mental deficiency, epilepsy, cataracts, cerebral sclerosis, congenital deafness, dwarfism, optic and peroneal atrophy, muscular dystrophy, megalocornea, Menkes syndrome, mitral stenosis, myopia, night blindness, nystiagmus, Parkinsonism, progressive bulbar paralysis, spinal ataxia, and many more.

In addition to female chromosomal defects expressed mostly in otherwise genetically sound males, men are also vulnerable to twice as many diseases as the female, and for the same reason. Acoustic trauma, acute pancreatitis, and Addison's disease attack men almost exclusively. Amoebic dysentery occurs in males fifteen times more frequently than in females; arteriosclerosis occurs two-and-a-quarter times more often; skin cancer is three times more prevalent among men, cancer of the pancreas, four to five times more prevalent; cerebral hemorrhage is monopolized by men; men suffer schizophrenia three times as often: and pregnant women who become schizophrenic within one month of conception, have female babies only (male babies are miscarried). Men suffer cirrhosis thrice as much as women; coronary sclerosis, twenty-five times more often; coronary insufficiency, thirty times; gout, forty-nine times; tuberculosis, twice as often. Autism is a preponderantly male affliction. Some of these diseases may have complications attributable to the way men make their living, but I have tried to omit some of the more obvious ones related to job overstrain.

Perhaps the most decisive evidence that the female double X has greater durability than the male single Y, is the fact that girls survived the bomb of Hiroshima better than did the boys. More girls exposed to it grew up normal, more boys were crippled. There is no other explanation than the genetic one. The bomb was ruthlessly democratic; it fell on men, women, and children alike. But more females survived it than males. The grisly experiment was conducted on such a massive scale that all other variables were wiped out. The only explanation that remains is that the XX combination had more survivability than the XY. As Montagu states, "To start off life as a male is to start with a handicap." This, he allows, is due to "inferior" male chromosomes. Yet most of the defects he lists are found on the female chromosome, and must be, as the female chromosome is a truck designed to carry the genetic load, while the male is a racer reserved for a few crucial duties.

The luck of arithmetic visits the defects on the male. It is one of the prices he pays for being commander and chief risk-taker. There is scarcely any dispute that the burden of survival has been placed upon the male. The female has been generously compensated for her secondary role by being given more safety and security, and the male has been properly penalized for his greater freedom and authority.

That the male has been genetically programmed for risk-taking shows up repeatedly. Between 120-150 males are conceived for every 100 females. Yet more males die *in utero,* since at birth there are only 106 American males for every 100 females—an excess of males over females so constant that it cannot be due to chance. In the great collection of human embryos at the Carnegie Institute in Washington, D.C., there are more male than female embryos, at every stage of development old enough to display sex differences.

After birth, the story remains the same; males still die off faster. In the first year of life, according to the 1946-48 statistics, three males died for every two females. By about the twentieth year of age, the greater attrition of the male has brought the two populations into balance, so that there are just enough to mate and reproduce without any leftover females.

But by age 21 there are fewer males than females—almost two males are dying for each female. At age 35, 1,400 men are dying for every 1,000 women. At age 50, women outnumber men 100-85. At age 55, men are dying at the rate of 1,800 per 1,000 women. And at 85, there are twice as many women surviving as men—striking evidence that men work too hard, take too many risks, and are genetically expendable.

At birth, life expectancy for women is better all over the world, in the poor countries as well as the rich ones. In 1950, there were 1,430,000 more marriageable females than males in the United States. In 1960, there were 2,700,000 more. At this writing, in 1970, there are 3,500,000 more.

These statistics are not only true for human populations, but are also roughly true for the greater part of the mammalian world. It is part of the grand design. Males are expendable risk-takers in the animal, as well as the human, world. The female has been allocated the easier task of risk-avoidance.

This explains the *why* but not the *how.*

The *how* is explained by the simple fact that since most of the genes are piled onto the female chromosome, the female chromosome is heavier, the male one lighter and smaller. Thus the Y-carrying sperms have a lighter load to carry, which gives it a slight advantage over the X-carrying sperm in the race to fertilize the egg.

Whatever the method, it is certain that more males are needed. For in addition to those that are going to be killed off in risk-taking, and have to be replaced, others will die from chromosomal defects and sickness.

We must now consider the relative risks each sex took as it reached maturity over the millenia. Although strictly speaking the risks men take have nothing to do with genetic quality directly, they do have an indirect effect on the quality of the genetic material being passed on from generation to generation, and can therefore be legitimately considered here.

Among the many valid criticisms that have been leveled against the deeply ingrained human habit of making war, not the least important is the observation that in war, it is usually the cream of the crop that gets killed off. The Achilles and Homers are eliminated before they have a chance to sire young, leaving the epileptic, the color-blind, and the flatfooted, to replenish the genetic pool.

In this century alone, war casualties run into many millions. On this scale, war is surely eliminating the best genes and propagating the worst. Instead of survival of the fittest, the formula seems to be death to the fittest and survival for the weak, at least as far as physical endowment is concerned. One dramatic example of this is the drop in the average height of Frenchmen by two inches, following the carnage of trench warfare. Unless one believes with Montagu that the biggest and most aggressive are necessarily the worst of the species, such examples furnish ample cause for alarm.

Yet, paradoxically, the grand slaughters of this century probably had no permanent deleterious effect on our genetic pool, since they caused hardly a ripple in our population figures. The decimation of World War I had been replaced by 1927—even though the French replacements, at least, were shorter.

But, though the critics got hold of the wrong war, they still have the right principle. It was in the small populations of the past, not the swollen agglomerates of the present, that the process of killing off the best and leaving the second-best to propagate, had its lasting effects.

In a tribe with fifty male adults, the loss of one outstanding young male has a more devastating effect than the loss of 500,000 does in a population of 100,000,000 males. In the small tribe the loss represented 2%, while in the larger group the loss of half a

million represented only one half percent. (My figures are illus-
trative only. I am not asserting that a loss of 2% will affect the
genetic pool while a loss of 0.5% will not. No one knows exactly
what rate is significant).

In 1930, while studying the Murngin, Lloyd Warner estimated
that in a population of 700 adult males, 200 deaths from fighting
occurred while he was there. At the rate of 28% that was
a genetic catastrophe. In New Guinea, in 1958, the Kapauku
took enormous losses in battle, as did the Marind Anim in
1966. In 1959, among the Fore of New Guinea, a death rate of
14% of adult males by ritual killing was recorded. Among the
Yanomamo of the Amazon a death rate of 24% from warfare has
been calculated, and the figure may err on the optimistic side. In
1805 the Blackfoot Indians of the Plains had a deficit of 50% in
their male population. More than fifty years later, in 1858, the
deficit was still unhealed at 33%, and the balance was not restored until the much later reservation period. In the valley of
Mexico, at the time of the Spanish Conquest, there was a death
rate of about 115,000 per annum out of an estimated population
of two million; 15,000 of these deaths were attributable to warfare
and human sacrifice.

The kill ratio among primitive peoples still living in the Stone
Age in places where no nation polices them, suggests that there
is much truth to the belief that in the past, warfare alone was a
major factor in human natural selection.

Consider the case of the flat-footed cave man. It is not only in
modern armies had such a man would be rejected for combat
duty and thus preserved for propagation purposes. He must have
been just as decisively rejected by the war and hunting parties
of the past, where fleetness of foot was vital.

Or consider the color-blind or near-sighted cave man. Could a
man unable to distinguish red from green be a proficient signal
man? Could a man unable to pick out a distant foe be an asset in
surprising him? Would he not have been relegated to supporting
roles while the fleet and the sharp-eyed took the risks—frequently
with fatal results? This primeval 4F may have taken second place
to the hero at tribal celebrations, but he was likely to be around
more often on those cold winter nights when human loneliness
cried out for companionship and warmth. Thus, it was likely to
be his genes, rather than the hero's, that most frequently sired
the next generation. And, given the promiscuous nature of the
supposedly monogamous human animal, does not the man with
the most opportunity seduce the greatest number of women?

Let us consider the epileptic. Far from being a necessarily undesirable mate, even today, the beliefs of the primitive made him a highly prized partner. Epileptics were thought to have magical powers and became witch doctors and shamans with great prestige. Epilepsy, which is frequently accompanied by superior mental endowment, can thrust its host into a high status position, which has never been a drawback in mating. The genes of the epileptic have probably been favored in human history.

Conjectures such as these have a strong intrinsic probability of being correct. There is also the additional fact that hazardous occupations are exclusively male occupations. Cave-ins in coal mines don't kill women, nor do women fall from bridges or skyscrapers during construction.

On the other hand, while warfare was lowering the quality of the genetic pool below what it could have been, in terms of physical endowment, it didn't diminish the intensity of human aggression; wars grew steadily bigger and deadlier. But if aggression was increasing, or at least holding its own, while general physical quality deteriorated, what was causing the increase?

It could only have been hunting. Evidently hunting was not as hazardous as war. Though some of the most aggressive would be killed off young, before they had a chance to acquire experience, this didn't happen often enough to dilute the pool of genes for aggression.

The survivors would be the richest or most powerful men, and have access to the most desirable women. They could support more offspring because of their greater ability to bring home the bacon. Thus, in the selection for aggression, we may have been getting the very best rather than the second-best. We may be getting better and better at aggression while our feet get flatter and our vision dimmer.

Until recently, geneticists felt they could add little to clarify the subject of male domination and female subordination. All they would say was that the chromosomes controlled the direction of sexual differentiation by triggering the glands into secreting more of one kind of hormone than another. As far as they knew, there was no genetic evidence to support either greater male aggression or male domination of the female. Such aggression as existed, they declared, had to be explained at levels of organic organization higher than genetics.

Cautious geneticists are still adhering to this position, although recent research has radically altered the evidential balance in favor of a genetic basis for aggression, from the lowest mammals up to, and including "plastic" man!

The Y- or male-determining chromosome evidently does more than choose sexual type and development—it also programs males for aggressiveness. The Y chromosome, through a particular gene not yet identified, declares that the male organism is an aggressive one, with attitudes commonly called *masculine,* which include the impulse to dominate the female. Aggression in human males is not simply a matter of conditioning; culture may add to it by emphasizing it, but culture does not put it there.

We have known for some time that the surface of the Y chromosome contains genes that have no counterparts on the X chromosome. One or more of these must be the aggressive ones, and two recent discoveries lend support to this theory.

The first critical evidence that he is programmed for aggression comes from a study of the lowly killifish. We have already mentioned that chromosomes sometimes fail to pair properly, which either kills the fetus or results in some kind of abnormality. A single X chromosome, unpaired, for example, might create a female with breasts but no ovaries or uterus. A single Y, we said, could not survive at all, though several kinds of abnormal pairings can survive. Sometimes the infant is an XXY, sometimes an XYY. There are even cases of XXYY's surviving.

But Dr. James Hamilton of the Downstate Medical Center in Brooklyn, New York, has gone nature one better. Though a single fetus will not survive in nature, Dr. Hamilton has succeeded in creating YY killifish in the laboratory! This creature is strictly a biological "sport" which cannot reproduce itself, but it provides crucial evidence that the Y chromosome carries one or more genes for aggression.

Dr. Hamilton took normal XY male killifish and reversed their sex in the usual way, by dosages of female sex hormone sufficiently heavy to suppress all male hormone production. The sexually reversed males, now female, were mated as females with other, normal, males. Some of their offspring were YY "supermales," a creature unknown in nature.

The next step was to introduce one normal XX female, one normal XY male, and one sportive YY supermale, into a common tank, let nature take its course, and observe the results. As expected, the normal male and the supermale began to compete for the right to mate the female. The result was epochal: In 155 tests the YY supermale won 137 times, to the normal XY male's eighteen! The fish that proves dominant in these contests is the one that, in a battle of swift darting and nipping movements, drives away the other and grasps the female with his fins, which stimulates her to lay eggs which he then fertilizes. In these competitions, the supermale induced egglaying almost all the time, and did more chasing, lunging, and self-asserting in the process. The tests were conducted with many killifish, not just one, making the resutls statistically certain.

A cautious scientist, Dr. Hamilton would not state definitely that the supermale was more aggressive, but he did admit that he was more competitive. Nor would he draw parallels between his findings and similar evidence of genetic aggression in human males. He has not yet determined beyond doubt whether the Y chromosome caused its effect directly, or indirectly by stimulating more sex hormone production. Either way, it is biological and thus innate.

Whether the genes of the Y chromosome control aggression directly, or indirectly by monitoring hormonal production, the variable is the extra Y chromosome, which causes aggression. The conclusion fits the other evidence. The supermale is more than competitive; he is overloaded with the type of aggression we are directly concerned with here, the kind that stimulates a member of a species to attack its own brethren, either for territory, dominance, or sexual possession; the kind of aggression which, in humans, is responsible for war, murder, and the domination of male over female.

Its presence in a creature so far down on the evolutionary scale indicates that it is not social in origin. And since it has such a basic function, we should expect to see it in higher types of creatures as well as in the lowly ones. That is precisely what we do see. The evidence for genetic aggression in man is as strong as it is for the killifish. In the course of evolution we have become adaptive with a vengeance, and have lost most of our innate drives, but not the aggressive one; this we share not only with the killifish, but presumably with many species in between.

Until now, one of the criticisms leveled against the claim of innate aggression in man, was that such aggression was being ethologically demonstrated for other species, such as rats, mice, and lions, and only *inferred* to hold for man also. Man's closest living relatives—the great apes, live in peace and rarely even fight one another. Considering the fact that even universal drives do skip species, this was a telling criticism. It was countered by pointing out that the great apes were herbivorous, whereas we had switched to carnivorous predation, and therefore could not rightly be compared to them. Only other predatory carnivores, no matter how distant, could provide valid comparison. We no longer need to fall back on this argument, because geneticists have recently come up with strong genetic evidence for innate aggression in man.

It has been known for some time that a sex chromosome abnormality is one cause of mental retardation in humans. (Recently this was discovered to hold true also for chimpanzees.)

In the general population, chromosomal abnormalities appear at a rate of about 0.2% for males, and 0.08% for females, i.e., two men out of a thousand and less than one woman in a thousand. But in institutions for the mentally subnormal, chromosomal defects are *five times* more prevalent—a full 1% for men and 0.4% for women, or ten men and four women out of every thousand.

If, for comparative purposes we add to the normal and mentally retarded groups, a group of mentally retarded who are also criminally violent, we find that the incidence of chromosomal abnormality *more than doubles* for the violent, as compared to the mentally retarded, and jumps eleven times as compared to the base group of normal men! The figure rises from 0.2% for normals to 1% for subnormals and 2.2% for subnormal violents. Other tests show even greater disparities. Yet, while the incidence of chromosomal defect increases for women retardates, from 0.08% to 0.4%, it increases only insignificantly to .49% for the subnormal who are also violent. This indicates that the X chromosome is not involved in female violence, which in turn means that the Y chromosome of the male is involved in male violence.

A group of geneticists then examined another prison population of mentally retarded, violent men, confined under conditions of maximum security, to see whether these results could be duplicated. They were not only duplicated, but unfortunately even improved upon: In this group, twelve out of 197 men had chromosomal defects—a total of 6%. Eight out of these twelve men, or 3.5% as against 2.2% for the first group, had an extra Y chromosome in an XYY configuration! To find a 3.5% incidence of extra Y chromosomes in a population of violent criminals, when in the general male population *all kinds* of chromosomal defects amount to only 0.2%, is to make an eye-opening discovery! Not only does the human male's Y chromosome carry genes for aggression, there obviously can be too much and too little of it. A double dose is more than civilized society can live with. Probably, too small a dose will be found to put men on relief rolls, but as of now this is just a guess.

How the gene works is not yet understood, but it may work by stimulating the production of the male hormone testosterone, which in turn triggers aggression. In one of the prisoners with an extra Y, a concentration of testosterone four times greater than normal was discovered. As we shall see later, male hormone in rats is definitely related to aggression.

The classic example of the human male with an extra Y chromosome, the mass murderer Richard Speck, behaves like a supermale killifish, only worse. The supermale did not kill.

Speck exhibits all three characteristics of the XYY male: tall height, low intelligence, and acne. (As acne results from unbalanced hormonal secretions it may be thought of as a secondary "sexual" symptom.) Tall height is so intimately connected to this chromosomal defect that in one group studied, a man more than 72 inches tall had one chance in two of being an XYY.

Behaviorally, the XYY human male displays extreme spacing aggression as well as marked sexual aggression, just like the supermale killifish. Speck not only demonstrated his abnormal aggression by murdering eight women in cold blood at one time, but also showed his hypersexuality by sexually molesting one of the victims. Before he perpetrated this ghastly crime he had a record of forty arrests and a history of violence against women. Other murderers show the same chromosomal abnormality profile.

While the killifish aggression was definitely innate, there is the possibility that the XYY aggression is not innate but "social," since the extra height, low intelligence, and bad complexion make the XYY male a social misfit. His resultant feelings of insecurity, fear, and antagonism stimulate him to react more violently, thus making his aggression the result of a hostile environment.

If this were our only evidence concerning human aggression, we might have to suspend judgment pending the accumulation of additional facts. But we already have more facts from many different sources concerning man's innate aggression, and this evidence tallies with all the rest. Not to read it that way would be bending over backwards to avoid the obvious; the genetic explanation accounts for more phenomena with less guesswork.

Doubt has been sown in laymen's minds concerning the correct reading of the genetic evidence, by the fact that the courts would not admit such evidence, thereby relieving Speck and his kind of responsibility for their acts. The layman rightly reasons that if Speck's aggression was innate he couldn't help himself, and should not be held responsible. But the layman doesn't know that the evidential requirements of a criminal court and a scientific laboratory are two different things. The evidence required by the court is *specific* and assumes free will on the defendant's part. The evidence required by the thinker is *general*; he does not concern himself with free will and determinism.

The evidence of an extra Y chromosome in Speck's cells, while strong enough to point to the *statistical probability* of aggression in Speck, was not certain enough to establish that he didn't know the difference between right and wrong. He may have had the urge to kill and *still known* that the urge was wrong. Evidence was merely offered to show that he was innately aggressive. But most of us are, and manage to restrain it. The social thinker must use the best information at hand at the moment of decision. He cannot wait for perfection. To the principle of Occam's Razor, of choosing the simplest explanation, there must be added the Navigator's Imperative—to use the best information at hand.

The social thinker does not have the responsibility for proving the guilt or innocence of any particular aggressor, and deals only in general laws or principles applying to the mass. Within this framework, there is no question that the evidence for genetically caused aggression in man, in line with the genetically caused aggression in many other species, should be made a basis for social judgment.

But before good Christians despair and conclude that war, murder, and rape are inevitable, let us understand the evidence correctly. Like the supermale killifish, the extra-Y human male is strictly a biological sport. Since he is abnormal, his actions provide no legitimate standard of expectation. His utility lies in the fact that his extremism allows us to detect the presence of genetic aggression as a normal endowment. Speck has a double dose of aggression, the rest of us have only one dose. The single dosage will fluctuate in intensity from individual to individual, and under extreme stimulus may make a Ghengis Khan out of a Milquetoast. But only special conditions would produce such behavior. Unfortunately, we seem to have absentmindedly provided such conditions quite often.

Not every human male with an extra Y chromosome is in jail for violence. Nor did the supermale killifish kill his normal competitor, or even win invariably. Probably the majority of human males with an extra Y simply has more "gall" than the rest of us, and in our society is probably more successful. Just as aggression does not inevitably doom men to savagery, it does not inevitably doom women to slavery. In line with the immense variability of individuals in any species, there are women who are more aggressive than men. And even among the normally un-aggressive ones, few are incapable of protecting their offspring from violence by returning violence. Even fewer are incapable of verbal aggression. And one need only watch the high-powered performance of some female entertainers to realize that the female sex has been given its measure of aggression too.

Those who doubt the interpretation of aggression propounded here may take comfort from such a skeptic as Ashley Montagu. One of the basic ideologists of the feminist movement, he has declared that there are no differences between male and female biology that warrant differential social status. Yet even he has been forced to admit the Y chromosome's greater "aggressiveness potential," and the X chromosome's greater "gentleness component." In the same article, written some fifteen years after his promulgation of the feminist party line, he admits that "there now can be very little doubt that genes do influence, to some extent, the development of behavior," and that "in some cases the additional Y chromosome exerts a preponderantly powerful influence in the genesis of aggressive behavior."

How he can admit this influence upon male behavior, and simultaneously maintain that there is no significant biological difference in the behavior patterns of male and female leading to masculinity and femininity, remains to be explained. It would seem necessary that he reconcile the difference and admit that the position he espoused in *The Natural Superiority of Women* has been rendered obsolete by the march of science.

The Message From the Glands and Gonads

When Dr. Hamilton was breeding his supermale killifish, an essential part of his method was to suppress normal hormone secretion and administer the hormone of the opposite sex. To manipulate hormonal secretions in this manner is standard operational procedure for animal breeders, endocrinologists, experimental psychologists, etc., though the public is not much aware of it. Through this type of experimental alteration of glandular secretions we derive our knowledge of the relationship between sex hormones and aggression. Aggression can be stimulated or inhibited by such manipulation, and thus can be observed directly.

Glandular secretion is initiated by a signal from the genes. Once the genes have determined the sex of a fetus, and endowed the male choice with a smidgeon of aggression, their task of building in characteristics is greatly aided by the endocrine glands, particularly in the matter of secondary sexual characteristics. In reality the action of the genes and glands are intricately related and are, indeed, inseparable; in principle, however, their functions are quite discrete and can be sharply differentiated: The genes function at the ground floor level and build *primary* characteristics. The glands function in the upper stories and build *secondary* characteristics, and generally elaborate the basic design. The glandular level, then, is the next higher level of organic organization.

With respect to aggression, especially sexual aggression, the glands supplement the action of the genes; they not only continue physiological differentiation into male or female sex, but also continue behavioral differentiation into masculine or feminine.

The male hormonal secretions add a stiff jolt of aggressiveness to the male, above and beyond that which was contributed by the genes.

During the first weeks after conception, the decision of the genes concerning the sex of the fertilized egg, or embryo, is not yet clear. To the eye, the sex of the embryo is indistinguishable. Each embryo has the same two features: a sex gland—or gonad— and a tubercle. About the sixth week, the gonad develops into either an ovary or testes, and the tubercle develops into either a clitoris or a penis. After birth differentiated growth continues apace, the very last phase of differentiation not taking place until the child has grown to puberty. At that time the ovary or testicle starts secreting hormones, as do other glands, thereby completing the process of differentiation.

However, it should be understood that in the male body the testes do not secrete pure male hormone alone, nor does the female body secrete pure female hormones only. Each sex secretes both male and female hormones, in complex proportions which make one sex major or dominant and the other minor or recessive, in the organism. Thus, sex reversal is always an open possibility; each sex has the intrinsic capacity to be the other, and sometimes becomes the other. This event can take place naturally or it can be induced surgically. Normally, of course, the sexes remain differentiated, the possibility of reversal never being more than a potential.

The process of differentiation goes much further in humans than it does in the lower orders, and continues right on up through the personality. The distinctions created are far greater than those which can be created by gene action alone. The genes rough out the primary sex characteristics, but the glands handle the refinements of secondary characteristics. They control the skin, musculature, bone, blood, and hair; they affect the very tissue itself, as well as initiate emotional and behavioral patterns. Despite the fineness of this differentiation, however, controlled observation can still detect the recessive presence of the other sex.

So far, six varieties of male hormones have been identified, grouped under the term *androgens*. Undoubtedly there are others. The chief of the known ones is testosterone, a product of the testes. When it is activated at puberty, it stimulates the growth of hair on the face and in the crotch and armpit; it enlarges the larynx and deepens the voice; it broadens the shoulders and continues the development of the bone structure; it vitalizes the prostate gland and seminal vessels. It is also responsible for the new erectile capacity of the penis and for the capacity to create sperm. Under the stimulus of testosterone secretion, the sex drive takes over the boy's mind, and "wet dreams" begin. Driven by unrelieved sexual tension, the boy displays increased aggression of the sexual kind, as well as increased intraspecific aggression.

The female hormones are grouped under the heading *estrogens*. Estradiol is the most crucial of the estrogens, and progesterone is an important runner-up. At the appropriate time they precipitate puberty and stimulate the development of the secondary sex characteristics associated with the female. The hips broaden, the breasts fill out, and menstruation begins. Less noticeable changes occur in the skin, mucous membranes, skeletal structure, and the water balance.

But, as already indicated, the hormonal secretions go farther than producing physical differentiation and start the distinguishing masculine and feminine behavioral traits as well.

In the young male the pressure of sperm production creates a tension that seeks reduction through discharge. He masturbates and seeks out the natural receptacle for his discharge—the female. His aggression increases noticeably. He smarts under parental restrictions which inhibit this aggression, and displays that first hostility to the father which will eventuate in his breaking away from parental authority and domination, so that his own initiatives can find expression.

This process is culturally encouraged in the blue-collar class, by the expectation of the parent that the boy go out and work. The prolonged financial dependence of the middle-class boy going on to college inhibits this breakaway, but he usually forces the break anyway, *against* the grain of his culture. The tension caused by unremitting sperm secretion drives the young man into behavior disapproved by his parents. So does his spacing aggression, which in its outward flow of growth meets parental restriction and is thereby further increased. At this stage of growth the parents cannot help but trigger the boy's hostility, and hence his aggression. They who formerly facilitated his growth now inhibit it, and their authority must be forcefully broken. Thus, the modern boy's behavior is going against his culture, and is not at all being caused by that culture. In primitive societies, however, this innate behavior is supported by *rites de passage*.

The young female is also changing under the impact of her glandular secretions, though her changes are not met by cultural hostility and are, in fact, usually explained as a result of cultural influences. But her behavior is really triggered by the onset of menstruation, widening hips, and enlarging breasts. As a child she was unconsciously aware of what she was made for, as her "inner space" patterns of thought indicate. But puberty forces this subliminal awareness to become conscious. This new conscious awareness makes her receptive to the male with a new intensity, even though she experiences no pressure comparable to that which sperm production produces in the male. A part of her consciousness turns away from external things and becomes permanently focused on her internal processes. The time has come for her to do her thing. She waits for it to happen, which gives her the appearance of inner passivity though she is energetic and volatile at higher levels of consciousness.

Just as we saw that *genetic* aggression is found at the lower levels of mammalian life as well as at the top of the heap in human males, so we will now see that *glandular* aggression follows the same pattern.

Male mice normally display marked spacing aggression towards each other by fighting a great deal. This aggression can be stimulated by rearing the mice in isolation and then putting them together in an environment of enforced socialization. When this is done male fighting is increased above the norm.

Yet when the male mice are castrated before puberty, thereby preventing the onset of normal hormonal secretions, fighting does not take place at all—except under one condition: When these castrates are artifically injected with the testicular hormone they have been deprived of, they will begin to fight. Obviously, therefore, their aggression was a product of their male hormonal secretions.

Manipulation of the female supports this inference. Like the female of other species, the adult female mouse fights only rarely. However, when female mice are injected with male hormone upon reaching maturity, they do fight. If drenched with the male hormone, they will fight savagely, even initiating attacks and seriously wounding their opponent. In one such case, the female actually killed her opponent.

Early injection of male hormone into the female not only creates a novel aggression in her, but also actually results in physical virilization. The vaginal opening becomes smaller and the clitoris hypertrophies. In other words, in mice, physical maleness and aggression are simply different aspects of the same thing.

This is further illustrated by a complementory experiment—injecting female hormone into the young male and suppressing his testosterone production. This reduces his fighting by fully 50%. It also scales down his sexual organs, which become lighter in weight and smaller in size.

Again the conclusion is inescapable that aggression is a function of the male hormonal secretion as well as a function of the Y chromosome. What used to be called feminine passivity is no more than the absence of this extra dose of aggression. But *lesser* aggression is not, as we have stated, tantamount to *absence* of aggression.

This lesser aggression produces a creature that fights and competes less because it has less need to fight and to compete. It has been endowed with just the right amount of aggression needed to survive in its niche. This is a general characteristic of non-predatory female mammals, as exhibited in their behavior. Predatory female mammals of course display more, since they hunt. (Even they, however, still defer to the male in non-predatory, social situations.)

Chickens furnish us with another vivid example of the relationship between aggression and glands. One can remove the ovaries from a hen and transplant male testes, which will grow and secrete male hormone. Upon maturity, the transsexed female is indistinguishable from a normal rooster. The bird will pursue females and will copulate with them in the male mode, like a natural male. However, it will be unable to reproduce, because it has no ducts along which the sperm could travel towards ejaculation.

The interference of man is not always necessary to bring about such sex reversal in chickens. It can occur spontaneously, especially among older hens. When it does, they begin to crow like roosters, develop rooster plumage, and pursue and mate with other hens.

Disease is the cause of such spontaneous reversal. It destroys the outer or female layer of ovarian tissue, leaving some of the inner, or male, tissue intact. The normal regenerative powers of the body cause the remaining male tissue to grow. Eventually the male hormone is secreted, causing the sex reversal to take place.

In at least one other recently discovered case, disease is not a factor in producing sex reversal. The absence of one sex and the overabundance of the other alone is enough to cause reversals. Females of the fish species *Anthias squamipinnis* can become males if there are no males in the school. When groups of twenty females were experimentally isolated from males, one would reverse itself into a male. When this new male was removed from the aquarium, another male developed from the remaining nineteen, and so on until twenty males had developed from the original twenty females.

We no longer need to remove the testes or ovaries from higher mammals by surgical methods in order to reverse their sex. Large dosages of estrogen will suppress testosterone production and stimulate the development of secondary female sex characteristics, such as breasts, in human males, as well as in other species. When this happens, the creature usually becomes less aggressive behaviorally. Changes of primary sex characteristics, such as transforming a penis into a clitoris, cannot be achieved by this method. These organs were developed by gene action at an earlier phase of growth and cannot be reversed by gland actions.

It is a truism for animal breeders as well as laboratory experimenters that administering male sex hormones to genetically true females tends to make them more aggressive. As aggression is a behavioral characteristic, it is obvious that the glands influence behavior as well as physique.

We have established that male sex hormones stimulate aggression in the lower mammals. If it is also true of man, we will realize once again that we are dealing with a general mammalian phenomenon.

It *is* true of man as well: Man is not so plastic that he has lost contact with his general mammalian past. He is at the end of an unbroken continuum. We have evidence of spontaneous hormonal malfunction in humans, the evidence provided by eunuchs, and that provided by a few thousand artifically induced sex reversals.

The rare female suffering from an excess secretion of male hormone usually signals this by a deepening voice, growth of hair on the face, and unusual preoccupation with sex, as well as an unusual display of aggressiveness. When this condition develops after she has reached adulthood, it is usually corrected by booster shots of female hormone. Once her true female balance has been restored, her voice gets lighter, growth of facial hair ceases, and she returns to her normal, less libidinized, less aggressive, self.

But when the condition begins early in life, before she has established all the female characteristics, and goes untreated too long, it may be impossible to undo the damage. She may have built secondary male characteristics before reversal is attempted. She is then akin to the adult male homosexual who wishes a sex reversal. His testes and penis can be removed surgically, and his breasts can be made to swell through female hormone administration; but he cannot develop ovaries.

Defects in the secretion of the female sex hormone can be matched on the other side, although there is nothing spontaneous about the eunuch. This ancient phenomenon of Oriental culture again illustrates the connection between maleness and aggression, by the lack of aggression where maleness is aborted.

When the testes are surgically removed from a young boy of prepuberty age, the boy never develops the characteristics commonly associated with maleness. The larynx does not grow larger, the voice remains high-pitched. The shoulders don't broaden, nor does adolescent aggression develop. As no sperm is created, no tension drives the boy into aggressive displays, and of course he develops no real interest in the opposite sex. Removal of the ovaries from an immature female also results in a failure to develop secondary sex characteristics such as breasts and broad hips, unless female sex hormone is artificially administered.

Strictly on the basis of glandular considerations alone, we can say with confidence that nature intends biologically true males to become masculine and aggressive, and biologically true females to become feminine and more passive. When this does not happen we are faced with a sport. Perhaps we would have all been better off had gender been made to follow sex *inexorably,* with no possibility of external circumstances overriding biological programming. But nature left the override option open and accepted some indeterminacy. As a consequence we have the phenomenon of the genetically and glandularly true male who is an emotional female, and vice versa. Flexibility has been maintained, the sport has not been destroyed, but human types are created who cannot reproduce themselves.

Sexual differentiation is not so sharp as it seems. Each set has the potential of the other in its makeup. The most male man has nipples, and his mammaries can be made to swell by injection of female hormones.

We are now moving into the area of gross anatomical differences and elementary behavior beyond the aggressive, which means we have escalated to another level of observation and discussion. The remaining evidence that males are programmed for aggression and dominance over the female, is neither genetic nor glandular, but anatomical and psychological. But nothing has changed ex-

cept our perspective. What was started by the genes and continued by the glands, is carried further still by anatomy and psychological processes. None of these can be attributed primarily to
culture, though they are all affected by culture.

Perhaps future research will decide that the effects I have here
presented as genetic are glandular, after all—that the genes have
worked not directly but indirectly by stimulating male hormone
production which in turn controls aggression. If so, the innateness of aggression has not thereby been disproved. Any behavior
controlled by the glands is still innate, and sexual aggression,
as well as spacing aggression, is at once behavioral and biological.

Anatomy and Simple Behavioral Differences

When we view the individual human being in a perspective which allows us to see him whole, we find that differences begun at the genetic level and continued at the glandular level are elaborated still further. If we back off even more to take in the human being in the context of his nearest living relatives, we see how naturally humans fit into the overall mammalian pattern. It isn't so much that we're different as it is that we're just *more*.

Even the untrained eye can hardly fail to note that the most obvious difference between men and women is size. Among the mammals generally, the male is not only usually more aggressive than the female, but bigger and stronger as well. In this as in many other respects, humans are not exceptional but run true to form. But larger size carries implications, and it is a rule of thumb in the mammalian world that larger size and power are accompanied by domination, and this also holds true for man. Being bigger confers an insidious advantage: Men dwarf women psychologically as well as anatomically, though they do not pay much attention to being more powerful than women. Women are much more conscious of being smaller and weaker than men. They can be hurt by men, but men cannot be hurt by women, ordinarily. Being smaller becomes an important factor in molding a woman's consciousness. They become aware early of not being able to do some things that men do without thought. Such awareness of limits to their horizons also encourages them to give up too quickly. The contrast makes them weaker than they actually are, and sets a pattern of not trying.

This limitation in size, and its effect on the psychological context within which women function, is unjust, undemocratic, and unequal. But it is, from a biological viewpoint, thoroughly right. Even in the world of the machine, men still perform all the tasks that call for muscle, because evolution has given them the requisite equipment. Perhaps now, with machinery displacing muscle, men will democratically shrink, and the scales of justice will be balanced. If this should happen, I rather think it would be the female who would be the first to decry it. She would then have nothing to look up to.

By refusing to take seriously the physical differences between the sexes, the neo-feminists shut themselves off from an understanding of the implications of those differences. These are profound. Unlike all other creatures on earth, who are specialists in some biological niche, man is a niche-less generalist. He owes his dominion of the earth to the fact that he doesn't belong anywhere in particular.

Man is not nearly as efficient at extracting energy from the vegetable world as the cow, who merely needs to bow its head to extract all the nourishment it needs from the earth. By contrast, man must hack away, plead with the gods, sweat, swear, and harness himself to a mass of machinery. In the matter of getting protein from meat, man is a clumsy buffoon compared to the lion. In the Arctic, merely to hold onto his own body heat consumes much of his energy. The polar bear is not even aware of the cold as a problem. In the sea, the minnows outswim man. In the air, man is a brick. In no dimension can man compete in efficiency with some other creature. In every slot he is a temporary occupant. Yet because he fits no slot well, he fills them all. The deer is on the land, the bird is in the air, and the fish in the sea, but only man is in all three.

Now, while our species owes its eminence to its generalistic orientation, the male of our kind is the most generalistic of all. The female is a specialist, in reproduction. The advance of science will make it possible to relieve her of this special task, if she wants to be, as males have been relieved of the task of exertion; but emotionally woman will still remain a specialist, as man will remain a worker.

Ashley Montagu disputes this notion that man is a more advanced evolutionary specimen than woman. His argument is a pedomorphic one. According to it, human growth has come about, in part, by slowing down man's development, by extending his stay in the womb, and by lengthening his years of infancy.

The prolongation of the formative period makes it possible for the child to absorb learning from his parents. He can accumulate far more knowledge through learning than his instincts would ever permit. Learning allows him to absorb the accumulated knowledge of generations of his species. In all other species, the brevity of infancy demands instinctual knowledge.

This much represents the collective wisdom of the specialists. Very few scholars dispute it. But the pedomorphic argument gives this chain of reasoning an additional twist, to the effect that the female is a more advanced type than the male.

According to the pedomorphic view, as presented by Montagu, human evolution is aiming at the human infant as its best specimen, rather than at the human adult. In other words, human progress is a progress in "youthification" rather than aging; and since the female skull is closer to the infant skull than the male, the human female is further evolved, evolutionarily speaking.

This argument, while highly provocative and stimulating, is also highly speculative, and quite wrong when it extends itself, on such slender evidence, as far as pronouncing the female more advanced.

Using precisely the same line of reasoning, blondes are more advanced evolutionary types than brunettes, because light hair is characteristic of babies; and Orientals are more advanced than Caucasians or Negroes because, like the baby, they have less body hair. Few would support these conclusions.

At the present state of knowledge, pedomorphism is too speculative to base pronouncements on; it is itself in need of validation. The obvious fact that the male body is the body of a generalist, while the female body is that of a specialist, is far more persuasive in the opposite direction. It is man's generality that has made him king. But woman is a far more committed specialist in reproduction and maternity than are her nearest female cousins in the simian world. On the basis of physiology alone, one would have to pronounce the male a more advanced evolutionary specimen.

But when all is said and done such arguments lead us backward rather than forward, into metaphysical considerations of superiority which deflect us from observation of available facts. Feminists cannot continue to ignore biological differences on pain of being irrelevant. No one who does not fully grasp the significance of the differences can be secure in efforts to mold public opinion.

We become so used to the differences between male and female at an early age, that in adulthood we tend to forget that such differences exist. But they are there, and some of the basic ones are ineradicable.

Machinery can go far toward redressing the disparity of performance power between the sexes, but it cannot change the emotional differences that are the proper accompaniment of the physical differences. Let us take a fresh look at these differences, and consider their possible consequences in the minds of man and woman.

Imagine the unclothed bodies of a man and a woman standing side by side.

This image demonstrates that, by rough judgment, the male body invests less than 5% of its mass in sexual reproductive fixtures. The genital area alone is devoted to that function, and the genitals are external to the body cavity, and free-swinging. They interfere in no way with other bodily functions.

By comparison, some 30-40% of the female's body mass is invested in, or seriously modified by, her reproductive function. One might caricature the female body as a reproductive apparatus with head and limbs incidentally attached.

These gross physical differences are not the only significant ones. There are others, less obvious, but still important to an understanding of the domination-subordination problem.

A most significant difference between the sexes is in the brain. I am not referring to the differences in size which occupied previous generations. Though the female has a slightly smaller brain in absolute terms, it may have greater weight in proportionate terms. There can be no question of differences in intellectual capacity, because the sexes are equal in brainpower.

But in women the cerebellum, or brain stem, or "old brain," is much larger than it is in men, which probably accounts for women's greater emotionalism. In biology, size is a function of use; what is not used atrophies. If the female cerebellum is bigger than the male's, it is because she uses it more. Other evidence supports this notion. It fits the observation that the female is the more cautious of the species. Risk-taking is an adjunct of the cortex.

Whether the larger cerebellum is in any way connected to the known chemical differences in the brains of the sexes, is not yet understood. But such differences there are, and we have to note them.

The female's more extensive use of her old brain may partly

explain why sex seems to come more naturally to the female simian than to the male. In some, though not all, simian species, it appears that the young male must see older males doing it before he can do it himself. A female chimpanzee, for example, can be brought up in isolation and still copulate without example or instruction; the young male brought up in isolation must learn how to go about it. Some species, such as, for instance, the Rhesus monkey, cannot be taught.

The fact that the male has to learn to do what comes naturally to the female, suggests that his learning brain, the cerebral cortex, or "new brain," is involved in his sexuality, whereas she is following the more instinctive and spontaneous directives of her old brain. If this is true, then masculinity has an intellectual component which femininity lacks. This seems to hold true for the lower mammals as well.

Another bit of evidence for this neural difference in sexuality is provided by the female rat, who will sometimes mount other females like a male. When her cortex is removed she ceases to mount other females in the masculine mode, but continues to be receptive to the male's advances and responds in the feminine mode. It is as though the masculine mode were cortical and the feminine mode went through the cerebellum.

That this neural difference may be true for humans as well as for lower simians is suggested not only by the female's larger cerebellum—which must be resisting transfer of the sexual function to the cortex—but also by the fact that homosexuality ("learned," and therefore cortical behavior) is more prevalent among males than females. True, the stimulus for retreat from the demands of the sex role is much greater for men than for women, and could account for the greater degree of male homosexuality; but it is also possible that the homosexual has made a "mistake," because his sexuality is more learned than instinctual. Certainly the role reversal of the "Bull-Dyke" lesbian is a lot less complicated than that of the male homosexual. This lesbian is always dominant to her "feminine" partner, while the male homosexual sometimes is and sometimes is not. One can infer nothing about domination and subordination from the outward appearance of most homosexual couples. In one relationship the homosexual may be dominant, in another he may be subordinate. Or such a relationship can sometimes be equal (the only case, perhaps, of a truly democratic relationship between two people who are not strangers). It is entirely possible that while the sex life of a lesbian is more complicated than that of a heterosexual, that of the male homosexual is even more complicated than that of the lesbian because of the cortical nature of male sexuality.

Another piece of evidence, this time from infant behavior, supports the thesis that the human male is more under the control of his cortex than the human female: The amount of activity displayed by the male infant varies according to the handling by the mother. But the amount of activity displayed by the female infant is independent of the amount of the mother's handling. The male is responding to outer stimuli, he is "learning." He is cortically controlled. The little female is independent of outer stimuli. She is more under the control of the cerebellum.

Why the cortex should favor masculinity and the cerebellum femininity is not at all clear—especially since the brain is so constructed that emotional impulses from the cerebellum flow through the symbolic impulses of the cortex and the cortical impulses in turn flow through the cerebellum, so that neither can respond in an uncontaminated way. But the evidence is there, and to the degree that the human mammalian male is more cortical than the female, though not more intelligent, he is further up on the evolutionary tree than the female. This, added to his generalist orientation, makes him a more advanced specimen than the female.

But Ashley Montagu is still not stopped. In further support of his thesis that the female is superior to the male, he presents the evidence that shows unequivocally that the young female scores better on all types of I. Q. tests than the young male. The usual inference that follows from higher and lower scores on intelligence tests is that one individual is smarter than another. Montagu makes the same inference—if females constantly score higher it is because they are smarter. Let us see.

Myron Brenton has estimated that there are over a thousand studies available on the comparative intelligences of the sexes. With the exceptions of mathematics, mechanics, and mazes, females achieve significantly higher scores on most of them. And concerning these three areas where they score lower, it must be acknowledged that they are the areas where girls are trained to defer to boys. As Brenton points out in *The American Male,* these exceptions are probably the result of training rather than natural aptitude. He quotes two studies which show that girls who happen to do as well as boys in these areas, have also been brought up to be more independent than the average girl. (1) Conversely, in areas where girls do best, in language and vocabulary skills, "badly overprotected boys," that is, boys brought up like girls, equal female performance. (2) (3) (4) Let us admit that the average school girl is two years ahead of the boy, as all experts agree, and dispense with further proof. What then? I have already claimed that the intelligence of the two sexes is equal.

A well known, but minor, reason which could account for this discrepancy is the exclusively feminine character of the school. In the boy's mind, learning is sissy and poor school deportment a proof of masculinity. Because the school environment is alien to his nature, the boy does not do as well, rebels more, and drops out more readily.

But the major rebuttal lies in the fact that this vaunted superiority disappears in adolescence—when the female gets ready for maternity. The moment a girl is physiologically ready for conception her mind stops growing. Conversely, the moment an adolescent boy begins to think of making a living, his I. Q. spurts ahead of the female's!

Can we claim "superiority" for him now? Obviously not. The better early performance of the girl was connected with the conservation of the species. Her nervous system developed faster in order to ready her for the breeding stage as quickly as possible.

The young boy has no such urgency of development. There are mature males around to take care of the girl's impregnation. His part in perpetuation is not as vital as hers. But once he enters the stage of preparing for his life's work, his I. Q responds and continues to grow until he and the girl live in two different worlds. The adult female, occupied with breeding, cannot compare to the adult, working male, in intellectual or emotional maturity.

Thus we have a case where girls do better in rehearsal; when the curtain goes up on the real thing the boy stars. If there is an element of superiority in this, as Montagu asserts, surely it must belong to the male. It is clearly better to be at maximum performance capacity in survival situations, rather than in training situations.

But given the direction of interest of the female at early maturity, it is doubtful that either sex is more intelligent than the other—even though the cerebral cortex plays a greater role in masculinity than it does in femininity. The female's job is retained by the cerebellum, where mistakes are less likely to happen. The male's job is kicked upstairs to the cortex. The cortex is the greatest, but it does make mistakes, and the use of it is risky.

Each sex is as logical and intelligent as the other, as well as emotional and intuitive. The female's task simply utilizes emo-

tion more and the male's task needs logic more. Women have the
intellectual resources if they are needed. And where the culture
calls for men to be emotional and intuitive, as contemporary
Iranian culture does, men have the resources to comply.

Early maturity, however, is the most critical stage for the modern woman, in a way it never was for her female ancestors. It is
at this point, where she has the option to assume a complete dependency upon the male, that she meets her hang-up. She can
use this dependency to hide from an unpleasant world, with a
perfect excuse for doing so. *It is my belief that this is precisely
what the mass of modern women are doing.* In avoiding independent careers and opting for the abnormal dependency of the
modern feminine role, woman is avoiding harsh reality and re-
treating into fantasy, with the apparent support of society. That
is why her intelligence stops growing when she decides to have
babies. The more aware she is, the more contact with unpleasant-
ness she has. By allowing her intelligence to atrophy, she can
pretend that the ugliness isn't there. *Modern woman has babies
as a refuge from a frightening world.* She not only has a baby, but
uses it as a shield between herself and the world.

It is possible that in this area woman is at a biological dis-
advantage: Her reliance on her cerebellum may make it more
difficult for her to concentrate than it is for men. With his usual
dexterity, Montagu presents this liability as an asset. "Women
are quicker to respond to stimuli," he argues, "both mental and
physical. In tasks involving rapid perception of detail and fre-
quent shifts of attention, women excel." In like manner he presents man's asset as a minor one. On tests measuring "reaction
to a single, expected, stimulus," males do better, he says.

Other investigators see this difference in a less tendentious
light. They note that this ability to concentrate on a single stimulus shows up early in boys. *He is much less distractable than the
little girl,* who must be held to her task, whereas the boy will
spontaneously keep on with what he is doing.

In fact, the difference is that between *clerical* skills and
problem-solving skills. Clerical skills are important, but not necessary to survival, either in the jungle of old or in today's business
jungle. The ability to concentrate *is* important to survival. The
ability to react to a single, expected stimulus, is a pendantic way
of saying that men can stick to a task until it is done. Man's
whole history can be seen in the light of this ability. Men were
made to face challenge. Women are more comfortable with rou-
tine administration, or housework, or nest-feathering.

But Montagu, it must be admitted, cites hard evidence to contradict this belief. World War II studies of the effects of English air raids showed that women took this kind of crisis better than men. Men more often suffered nervous breakdowns.

Yet this evidence is not as damaging to our thesis as at first blush it seems to be. We know that the double XX chromosome arrangement is stronger than the XY one. It not only survived the bombing of London better, but the bombing of Hiroshima as well. The dominance of men does not depend on greater ability to withstand shock or pain in a helpless, defensive situation; it depends upon his ability to take the initiative and stay with it until a crisis is resolved. Being able to "take it," emotionally, is a female asset, not a male one. She was made for durability. He was made to sprint.

There is no doubt that women generally can take pain better than men. They are conditioned to expect it from an early age. In this special case their ability to wait and endure gives them a toughness usually reserved for men. Men, not expecting pain, and not accustomed to waiting and enduring, are surprised by pain and respond to it with the tenderness usually associated with the feminine mode.

The bomb shelter evidence is further distorted by the fact that women are allowed to scream in terror under air raid attack. Men are not. They are supposed to meet crisis by holding on to their wits. Having to contain and suppress fear, they tend to break down later, when there is a medical statistician around to make note of it. In the bomb shelter, no one made notes.

This catalog of male-female differences goes on and on. They all suggest the same thing—that there are biological differences between the sexes which make equality an empty phrase.

The human female shares with her sisters of the lower mammalian orders a sense of smell much more acute than the male's. With the chimpanzee female she shares more dexterous fingers and a liking for dressing up in finery. Why the sense of smell should be better is not clear. Perhaps it is an accidental attribute of the old brain which the male has lost and she has not. It may be because she can, in the primitive state, smell changes in the condition of the infant. A possible clue is the fact that her keenness of smell fluctuates with the menstrual cycle, depending upon the amount of estrogen being secreted.

There are other clues to inborn differences, especially noticeable in infants and children. In general, boy babies are more restless than girl babies, and sleep less. Furthermore, the boys are

more restless *before* feeding, and fall asleep afterwards. Little
girls are quiet before feeding and get restless *afterwards*. This
trend seems to carry over into adulthood. The adult male tends
to fall asleep after the evening meal, while the female wants to
go out. But this can also be explained simply by the male's need
for relaxation after a day's work, and the female's boredom after
being cooped up at home all day.

With the greater restlessness of the boy goes a stronger explora-
tory urge, as would be expected of a future hunter. Girls play
closer to the mother and are hesitant to strike out, which is con-
sonant with their biological task of avoiding danger. In nursery
school, teachers notice that many *girls are more hesitant than
boys to play new games,* or to work at new tasks. But such timidity
can be relieved by assuring the girl that nothing important is
at stake, and that she will not be judged for her performance.
This behavior occurs at a time when her nervous system is already further developed than that of the boy of the same age.
Potentially, the girl should be better able to deal with the new
challenge than the boy.

Her timidity and the boy's adventurousness may explain her
greater aptitude for language. She is at her mother's side more
constantly, and talks more. He is away more and talks less. It is
interesting to note that when a coeducational class is broken up
into boy and girl sections, the boys show more interest in aca-
demics and the girls show more courage.

The boy not only displays more aggression by fighting, but
is also more likely to stutter and have emotional problems of
adjustment. The unavoidable frustrations of the learning process
also stimulate his relatively greater capacity for aggression. When
he expresses it he is allowed to get away with it more often, so
that it frequently beomes a habit with him, and he goes on to
tantrums and breaking things. At the age of one year he shows
more interest in mechanical things than girls. This was susceptible
to a cultural explanation until Erik Erikson performed his fa-
mous experiments with building blocks.

These boys and girls grow up and, regrettably, some of them
commit suicide. Even this they do in significantly different ways.
Women prefer sleeping pills. The big boys have a penchant for
violent endings and use the rope or the gun, or jump from tall
buildings.

Those individuals who prefer not to believe that humans are
innately aggressive, might take another look at the little angel in
the crib. A baby lying in a wet diaper is not merely frustrated

but frequently in a total rage. Desmond Morris quotes a study that declares that by the time an infant is four months old, aggression is a part of his repertoire. Before that age he merely indulged in a generalized kind of angry crying, brought on by frustration. But by the fourth month he can express temper tantrums, and does so. He attacks small things, shakes larger ones, spits, bites, scratches, and strikes out at the world. Little of this is suggested to him by cultural contact. Soon the baby develops facial expressions that appropriately express his emotions: he glares, frowns, and clenches his fists. Such infant responses are not peculiar to our culture, but are universal.

This catalog of innate differences between human males and females could undoubtedly be further expanded. But I think we have established that such differences do exist, and that they illustrate emotional differences beneath the level of cultural molding. The most striking proofs of such innate differences still lie ahead of us. All of this evidence points to the fact that the two sexes are not on a parity of power, or on a parity of function.

But again a word of caution is in order. The male dominance which the evidence indicates, is not absolute but relative. In a statistically significant population, male domination shows itself clearly. But individual by individual, some females are just as clearly more aggressive than some males.

Where, among simians, a female happens to be scrappy enough to dominate some males, she usually shows other signs of masculinity as well. In like manner, a subordinate male will show signs of femininity. For example, among the apes and baboons, a subordinate male may make a "sexual presentation" of his buttocks to the tough female. The female does not take this presentation at face value, as a sexual invitation. She understands it is a sign of submission. The same low-status male may make the same presentation to a dominant male, or a weak female may do so to a tougher female.

Obviously, the genetic inputs vary greatly from individual to individual. One male doesn't get the same dosage of aggression as another; some females get an excess of it. Even if the inputs were exactly the same, each dose goes to an organic system slightly different from the next one. But in large populations there is no question which way the twig is bent.

Surveys of the zoological scene make it glaringly obvious that male dominance is not a uniquely human invention, arbitrarily foisted upon country-bumpkin females by city-slicker males, but a practically universal convention.

One need not be a professional ethologist working in the wilds of Africa to see the principle at work. Anyone who keeps dogs or cats in pairs can observe it. I have reared both and have been repeatedly impressed by the fact that the female of both species is a comparative homebody, while the male is a wanderer. I have never had a female dog, not in heat, voluntarily stay away from home overnight. I have never had a male dog, not sexually stimulated, who didn't. Even older males, beyond the call of the flesh, like a few days of unscheduled freedom. Not only is the bark of a bitch higher, like the voice of the human female; I go so far as to say I have seen a female dog act shrewishly and a male cat act bossy.

The same differences obtain in the matter of obedience. The female dog rarely shows resentment of subordination. The male dog sometimes does. I have had a male dog, completely attached to me and never knowing another master, who would periodically refuse to obey me, apparently out of the sheer irksomeness of subordination. This dog had a hard core of individuality which he did not wish to surrender, though he was as affectionate and loyal a pet as I ever had.

The domination of the male cat over the female is even more unmistakeable. I have repeatedly watched a half-grown, four-months-old, male cat completely dominate four fully grown females twice his size, including his own mother. His domination displayed itself by cuffing and driving away the females from the food plate. He also made inspection checks on them at periodic intervals, as though looking over his property or harem. During such inspections he would frequently cuff them, for no discernible reason. They would not fight back.

There can be no question that in the higher mammals at least, the male is habitually more aggressive and dominant than the female, as well as larger and more powerful. An hour at the zoo will show that the male chimpanzee is far more aggressive than the female, and far less well behaved. It is true that the chimpanzee in captivity is more aggressive than the free one, but people who have kept them as pets note that even in freedom the male is more aggressive. He takes the initiative in play and plays rougher and harder. Among the monkeys the male not only plays rougher and with more initiative, but goes so far as to threaten the female with aggression.

The macaque monkey and the baboon will force an unwilling female into sexual congress in a manner strongly suggestive of rape. One can also observe the male housecat pouncing upon the female and forcibly gripping her by the neck with his teeth, to hold her steady for sexual entry.

There is nothing in this that is not recapitulated at the highest evolutionary level by the human male. At every level he has shown himself more aggressive, more dominant, more destructive, and more murderous than the human female. Environment, culture, education, or brainwashing, are not adequate explanations. Cultures don't create these differences in humans, any more than culture creates them in other mammals. Culture merely amplifies or subdues them.

At this juncture we have been getting into pure behavior, almost divorced from its physiological base. Paradoxically enough, it is in the very area of pure behavior that we get our strongest, most convincing evidence that male domination and female subordination are innate, inherited traits of biological origin.

The Feminine Psyche

Here and there in this study I have made passing reference to the fact that the emotional attitudes of women parallel, at a higher level, the physical uniqueness of women, and facilitate the enactment of their special role. The female's body and mind work together. In the study of life from simple to more complex forms, specialists frequently refer to the phenomenon of "displacement upwards." By this they mean that as an organism increases in complexity, functions once performed at a lower level move up and are performed at a higher level. To say that the female has a feminine mind is essentially to say no more than that. Given the emergence of a brain in a sex, the brain functions in the mode of that sex, in matters sexual. A brain in a male body tends to function in a way that we call masculine; a brain in a female body tends to function in a way we call feminine. Both modes clearly help to get the special job of the sex done.

A nine-months' pregnancy and a child dependent for several years barred the human female from the hunt, which in turn barred her from a supply of protein and a measure of aggression. The tactic she devised to overcome these deficiencies, which were female deficiencies, was a feminine one. She defaulted to the whole of the opposite sex, including those low-aggression males she could have dominated, and bound the opposite sex to her by attractiveness and magnetism rather than by force.

The human female needed the male much more than did her

simian sisters. The simian female needed the male for protection and impregnation only. The human female needed the male for that *plus* food. Being herbivorous, the simian female could supply her own and the infant's food by herself. But the carnivorous human female, who couldn't hunt, was in a bind. Thus, while the simian female was merely subordinate to her males, the human female was both subordinate *and dependent*—though not so dependent as the modern American female.

The human female accomplished the difficult feat of binding the male to her as a food supplier through sexuality and submission. It was by submissiveness first, which disarmed the male's spacing aggression, followed by the projection of allure, that the conquered one conquered the conqueror. Submissiveness she did not need to invent; millions of years of evolution had perfected it. For defeated males as well as for noncontesting females, submissiveness is the signal that turns off aggression in the dominant animal. The female merely institutionalized it. The feminine attitude is incipient in subordination.

Having turned off the male's aggression, the female next turned on his sexual appetite and bound him to her. The human female's capacity for orgasm is absolutely unprecedented, as is her receptivity. Other simian females are available only a few weeks out of the year. The human female is available almost all the time, and derives enough pleasure from the sex act to experience an orgasm which is totally unnecessary for reproduction. The point was not lost on the human male. He did not have to prowl the woods for receptive females when he had one at home.

Yet it was by the way the human female bound the male to herself that she forged her own chains, for the sexual woman is a woman naturally in surrender, naturally in subordination. And her diffuse and persistent sexuality does not permit her surrender to be sharply defined and limited only to sexual situations. It carries over into all aspects of the male-female relationship, as evident in the constant and unconscious deference she displays towards the male, which is paid for by restraint of aggression on his part.

Up to this point we have presented ethological, genetic, endocrinological, and anatomical evidence for the biological subordination of the human female to the human male, at least in intimate relations. By chance, this evidence has more strongly supported the secondary source of feminine subordination—spacing aggression, rather than the primary cause of subordination—sexual aggression. I shall remedy that deficiency now.

Before doing so, however, I would like to point out that it is the massive failure of the feminist leadership to recognize what every normal female knows in her gut—that women are sexually dominated—which ultimately vitiates all recent feminist ideology. It is lack of recognition of the part played by brute sex which makes the whole feminist demand for equality obsolete. Only one writer, Kate Millett, has recognized the part sexual aggression plays between the sexes; only she discovered this insight in literary materials and appended it to the concept of *power* rather than the concept of *aggression,* and thus was unable to make full use of it. Had she connected sexual aggression to aggression-thinking in general, and had she added to her insight the complementary one that the female welcomes aggression (selectively), she would have written another book than *Sexual Politics.*

The strongest evidence for sexual aggression in human males, other than that already set forth, happens to be psychological in nature and comes in two kinds.

The first is a study of the conventional sort, which pleases social scientists. The second is a powerful insight provided by psychoanalysis. Together they reveal that things commonly understood were not really understood at all, or only in the most superficial way.

In a study which by now has become a classic, Erik Erikson discovered that feminine identity is built on what he aptly calls "inner space." By this he means that woman's physical design harbors an inner pouch or space destined to contain offspring. (She also has another inner space designed to contain a penis, though Erikson does not refer to the vagina. Yet I would think that all which applies to the area intended to hold the growing fetus must also apply to the area intended to house the penis.)

Paralleling this somatic design, is a psychosomatic awareness of the design and what it signifies. In effect, woman's thought patterns seem to be an echo, on a higher level, of this somatic design.

Erikson's proofs of his thesis were accidentally arrived at while he studied boys and girls at play. He noticed that when playing with blocks, boys and girls used space differently. Certain configurations consistently occurred in girls' constructions, and other configurations consistently appeared in boys' constructions.

The girls almost always built scenes of house *interiors,* emphasizing *enclosed space,* in the form of *low buildings, inside* of which were figures of *people* in *static* positions. Mostly these structures were peaceful. But sometimes an *intruder,* animal or human, came into the scene. These intruders *were not feared.*

Instead, they brought an element of humor or *pleasurable* excitement into the picture. The only noteworthy architectural feature that might appear to relieve an otherwise monotonous scene, would be an elaborated *doorway*.

By contrast, the boys focused on the *exterior* of a building, creating *high* structures with phallic *protrusions*. Their figurine people were usually *outside* the house, and *in motion*. One other feature distinguished boys' scenes from girls' scenes: The boys' scenes frequently contained *accidents,* and buildings would periodically *collapse*. *Ruins* were almost exclusively a part of boys' scenes.

In other words, females were unconsciously concerned with safe, static, inner space. The boys were unconsciously concerned with lofty towers, motion, destruction, or outer space. The safety of the female inner space could only be breached through a doorway, by an *anticipated* intruder. Obviously, the respective modes of thought paralleled the morphology of the genitalia and symbolized biological mission.

Other observers, shown pictures of these play constructions without knowing who built them or why, matched the two types of constructions with the sex of their creators with statistically significant frequency. Two-thirds of the constructions were correctly identified as "male," and more than two-thirds were identified as "female."

These tests revealed much more than the already known fact that girls like to play house, and that boys are active, outward turned and destructive. The detail and depth with which psychological differences mirrored sex differences was astounding. The morphology of the mind, so to speak, was the same as the morphology of the body.

In the male we have an external, erectile organ which functions intrusively and invades the female inner space, sometimes tearing a hymen in the process, and there delivers motile sperm. There is access to the inner space of the female through a "doorway." Waiting inside is a statically "expectant" ovum.

Such parallelism could never have been produced by cultural conditioning. In fact, the environmentalists see nothing more in this behavior than that boys are active. Culture can condition a little girl to expect to be a mother, but it cannot condition her to build structures that mimic her own biological role. Nor can coincidence explain such an unbroken chain of parallels in both sexes. Only biological purpose can adequately explain the phenomenon. Each sex has reproduced in symbolic form its own sex role and life style. To those who doubt this interpretation Erikson replies with a question: If these results could have been obtained through conditioning, why did no boys construct scenes of sporting events? If girls are taught to play it safe, why were there no scenes of *high* walls and *locked* doors?

In the original instructions on how to use these blocks, the children were told to imagine themselves as film directors creating an exciting movie scene. Neither sex carried out these instructions. Both began consciously to do so and then forgot. Their work was taken over by unconscious forces. It was their unconscious minds that produced these play constructions, and their unconscious minds mimicked their procreative functions to the letter. Culture simply does not have that kind of accuracy. *Sexual function not only differentiates the sexes physically, but mentally as well.*

Erikson points out that the domination of the whole play space by the sex differences is like a "field" dominance. I might add that it is like a magnetic or electrical field, not simply an "aura," and far transcends mere symbolic representation of the sex organs. The boys' constructions were not simply phallic symbols, but *male modes of thought,* male modes of being. The male *is* action. He also *thinks* action.

The female inner space accounts for her fears as well as her hopes. In youth she fears not being married, not being "filled up." In later life, she fears being empty and unused. As a youngster the male fears "not making it." In later life he fears not having made anything lasting.

It is during pregnancy that woman most clearly displays features that lead to her description as passive, and thereby converted what was a relative thing into an appearance of an absolute. During pregnancy the female is inward turned, attuned to her own organic processes. This attitude has been labeled as passivity when, in fact, it was merely the special kind of activity appropriate for pregnancy. It is the female's business to provide the ovum with quiet and stability. Her body is a shelter between it and the storm. Like a gyro, she must translate outer motion into apparent stillness, to provide a quiet harbor in a raging sea. Her "action" is to stop action for the sake of the fetus. Her business is to stand still, but in order to do that she must constantly expend energy.

That this inner space of the female suffuses her mode of awareness, and is not a culturally produced phenomenon, is supported by a crucial fact of psychoanalytic observation.

Human males clearly demonstrate their inclination towards domination of the female in their fantasies and dreams. Perhaps the most common dream males experience is the dream of rape, of forcefully taking women.

At the same time, the female shows her inclination to subordination by fantasies of being enjoyably raped.

It is true that dreams incorporate everyday experience, and thus contain a cultural element. But the motive force or reason for the dreams' existence is not everyday experience. They are not culturally induced; in fact, they go against the grain of cultural indocrination and stem from the very depths of the psyche. The male's dream of sexual aggression and the female's dream of being enjoyably sexually attacked is as innate a phenomen as the dream of falling from a tree. If it were culturally produced then it should be absent in some cultures, but it is not. It is a true universal.

Even more conclusively, it is a fact that many females experience this fantasy or dream of rape before coitus is ever experienced or even before puberty sets in! And this imaginative experience is not a frightening one but a welcome one.

Though anthropologists have not systematically surveyed all the cultures for the prevalence of rape fantasies, enough of them have been documented to establish universality. For example, Margaret Mead found that Dobuan women dreamed of rape, and that Iatmul men and women talked about it constantly. Among primitive tribes the rape of female prisoners is a fairly prevalent practice, as for example among the American Plains Indians and the warlike tribes of New Guinea. Nor is civilized man exempt from this practice. There was a particularly gruesome case of American soldiers in Vietnam kidnaping a girl, gangraping her, and then killing her. One way in which Jewish women escaped incineration in German concentration camps was by serving in brothels. A much publicized motorcycle gang in California practiced rape as a normal event.

Fantasy, of course, has by definition nothing to do with reality. In fantasy the female has her choice of rapist, in reality he is likely to be a fearsome and repulsive man, who may also beat her; so the fact that men and women dream these dreams has nothing to do with their actual behavior. But it does tell us that male domination and female subordination stem from the very depths of the human soul.

In fact, all sexual intercourse may be regarded as more or less a form of rape, no matter how voluntary, and no matter how much love and tenderness is infused into it. The very mechanics of coupling require force. The penis must be firmly inserted and energetically pistoned, in order for ejaculation to occur. It is impossible to do this without a modicum of aggression. It is therefore impossible for women to learn to enjoy intercourse without simultaneously learning to like the unavoidable aggression that goes with it. But the pain inflicted by the inserted penis is not the same as the pain that comes from being brutally beaten and raped by an unwanted assailant. In enjoying thrusting into the woman, the male is being sadistic. He likes hurting her in that particular way, though he may be horrified at the thought of socking her. In welcoming his sexual aggression the female is masochistic. She likes being hurt in sexual combat, though she might be terrified at the thought of being beaten up. Sexual intercourse is an aggression, a pleasurable, welcome aggression, but an aggression nonetheless. Sex can be experienced without love. The closer a male moves towards orgasm the less loving and the more brutal he becomes. The closer the female moves towards orgasm the more she welcomes complete obliteration. The male moves more and more from the attitude of loving suppliant to the attitude of subjugating conqueror. The female becomes a compliant slave. Sexuality is a matter of pleasureable violence.

As the sexual act exhibits most clearly where social domination of the female originates, so within the sex act itself the orgasm shows itself to be the core of that phenomenon.

At orgasm the male is like an automaton, or like a man in a trance. His sexual act is almost a repetition-compulsion, a spasm as inexorably performed as his breathing. Until discharge, he is almost without power to stop. His being is taken over by his assigned biological task, to impregnate the female. As nature reserves to the instincts those tasks which most vitally need to be performed, so as man moves towards his climax he comes more and more under the domination of his reflexes. There may have been gentle solicitation at the beginning of the act, but as it moves towards culmination nature reveals her truth nakedly. The pelvic thrust is pure reflex, pure automatic action. He is injecting his sperm into her body by aggression. The method is brutal, and because brutal, absolutely certain. No qualm, no courtesy, no delicacy, no tenderness, is allowed to interfere with the delivery of the sperm to the ovary. By the *method of desire* nature brings the two sexes together; by the *method of aggression* nature makes absolutely certain that the waiting egg will be fertilized. In the sex act, love and tenderness are overlayers contributed by later evolution, because love and tenderness cannot insure the delivery of sperm to the egg. In fact, tender regard for the female may block impregnation.

It is in pornography that the hard core of the male-female relationship is most clearly exposed. As against the love of an Elizabeth Barrett and Robert Browning, pornography depicts the progress of the male from tender solicitor to brutal ravager, and the female from girl scout to unashamed wanton. *Pornography asserts that man is essentially a savage rapist and woman a willing victim.*

But welcome aggression is only the core of sexuality, not the whole of it, for humans. The human male's task is not simply to impregnate the female; he must also provide for the offspring, and has been tested for his reliability for this task by the female. He showed enough patience and staying power to court and woo her, to flatter and cajole her, to bring her gifts of food and promises of more. He promises to be reliable.

In the lower orders, the female has completed her task by the act of giving birth, or shortly thereafter. In the human species the task of mothering is not finished until the infant is mature. That is why the female employs attitudes which seem to defeat the end of impregnation, by holding the male off. But this is only temporary behavior, a screening device to test his durability. Her coquetry and flirtation attract him and stimulate his sperm production. Once he is attracted and in orbit about the female, the contrary biological tactic is brought into play. Having attracted him, she now repels him. If he endures, he might be counted on to stick around and provide food and shelter. Some males fly away. That is all to the good, biologically. They would not have been around to shelter the fetus they sired. The more frustration a male endures the more likely he will be to secure the survival of the offspring he will create. Once he has proved himself in this way, he can be let into the treasury. But the female may be so cautious and draw this phase out so interminably, that he may lose patience and resort to rape.

This behavior is of the essence of femininity. She repels and attracts, attracts and repels. She attracts impregnation but allows only durable males to impregnate her. In fantasy she can dwell on the pleasure of rape because that is the fundamental task. But in reality she must be practical and assure that the infant will receive shelter and food. The real rapist does not stay around to supply that, so real rape is not actually wanted.

The desire to rape and be raped is not a uniquely human phenomenon, but is distributed up and down the mammalian line. The male cat approaches the female sexually by stalking and pouncing upon her. Once straddled, he forcefully holds her in position by the scruff of her neck with his teeth. This is the cat's equivalent to rape at the higher human level. It is a form of behavior duplicated by many higher mammals. Male sheep bite the ewe's neck in sex play. The stallion bites the mare's neck while mounted. Even monstrous elephants hold the female in position by a bite of the neck. Bats and rabbits do it, as do sables and shrew, marten and mink. Particularly the mink. The female of this species puts up a battle. Her resistance is vigorous and prolonged. Active domination by the male seems absolutely essential to her.

It is the nature of mammalian males not only to be violent and forceful, but to inflict pain. Ford and Beach (5) have demonstrated that the violence the males of some species inflict in sexual intercourse has an important biological function. While in some species pain merely stimulates sexual desire, in others, *it is essential to impregnation.* If intercourse takes place without the required stimulus of conflict, conception rarely occurs.

The prevalence of this form of sadism as a sexual stimulant is not yet known. But it is definitely there, as was proved by controlled experiments with male rats. The copulation pattern of the male rat consists of a number of "mount bouts" at fairly regular intervals until orgasm occurs. Administering mildly painful shocks to a group of rats resulted in increasing the rapidity with which the rats made successive mountings. It also induced the rats to mount more often. In sum, a mildly painful shock increased the rats' sexual urge and performance.

What is true for the mink and rat may not necessarily be true for humans. But humans too show ample evidence that pain is a sexual stimulant, at least for some. The whip and the scourge are much in evidence in the world of professional sex. In Victorian England, according to the pornography of the age, whipping was practically a national pastime. While some humans who practice pain in sex may be perverted, others may not be. They may just be acting out of an ancient, if not particularly attractive, biological compulsion.

Ford and Beach maintain that "high levels of erotic arousal tend to generate moderately assaultive tendencies in the male of our species." Yet, though women may find the receiving end of a little pain enjoyable, they usually do not like inflicting it.

Woman's thing is masochism, and sadism is usually the province of the male. When we hear of an Amazon in spiked heels whipping some submissive male, she is usually doing it for hire or for accomodation, not for pleasure. But given the variability of our kind, a certain portion of the female sex is bound to find inflicting pain pleasurable. Normally, though, pain for the female is proof of subjugation. There are women who need this proof so badly that they will provoke and goad a man until he beats them. (After which they may have him arrested for assault!) Most women, however, are content with symbolic domination and do not like pain—they simply tolerate that amount of pain which is unavoidable.

The example of the woman who provokes assault, takes sexual pleasure in it, and then has the man arrested for it, is more than an amusing paradox. Here is a point where the different feminine roles collide, where contradiction prevails over internal harmony. In a democratic and Christian society no one has the right to subject others to force or violence. Yet in the totalitarianism of intimacy, the man who refuses to deliver violence to the woman who needs it, is a man who has failed her needs and has been delinquent in his masculine duties. That he is damned if he does and damned if he doesn't, is more than an exasperation; it is a failure of modern society to harmonize the demands of sexuality with the requirements of civilized living. It is an extension of Christian-democratic thought into areas in which it has no business being.

Democratic theory and Christianity must face up to the sexual core of the human personality. In sex we are neither equal, nor "nice." But we are complementary. In sex man is an aggressor and woman a wanton. Christianity and democratic theory find this fact unappetizing and uncongenial, as well as tending to contradict its beliefs in the goodness of human nature. Not being able to resolve the contradiction, the theorists have distorted and muffled it under layers of love and tenderness.

Why Christianity acts this way is a fascinating story, but one whose detailing falls outside the scope of this study. To summarize, males and females are people as well as males and females, and have other relationships besides sexual ones. Because the whole of the human personality is not expressed in sex, love, tenderness, and brotherly consideration became imperatively needed organizing principles of behavior, once city life and mass populations came to dominate the human scene. Earlier man, of course, expressed tenderness in the relationship of parent and child, etc., but he had no need of articulating love as a principle of behavior. Yet when Neolithic man came together in great cities he had need to enunciate principles of legitimate behavior. He was now living with strangers, rather than familiars, and rules were needed. It was worth any price to articulate these ideas, and to install them as rules of conduct in this new beehive. It was difficult to do so and the price paid was high. In order to get these ideas in, others had to be kicked out, and the baby was thrown out with the bathwater. Antagonistic ideas, as well as hostile behavior, had to be suppressed. All aspects of aggression were declared illegitimate and uncivilized, including the aggression of sexuality. It is now time to bring the two contrary claims on conduct into harmony. Tenderness must defer, in matters sexual, to the more primitive aspects of sexuality. The orgasm is not gentle, but it is splendid, and splendor is an experience humans need as much as kindness.

We should not feel that we are brutes or freaks, unable to escape our vicious past. To be alive we must remain corporeal. We must continue to be organisms, to have a past and a future—that is, to have some kind of structure and system.

Am I saying then, that the social scientists err in believing we have evolved beyond sexual differences, and that Freud was right in believing that "anatomy is destiny"? Basically, yes. But it is a complex yes, not a simple one.

Insofar as a woman is in intimate relations with a man or men, she is caught in a web of domination-subordination. The greater the intimacy the stronger the chains; the weaker the intimacy the weaker the bonds. With strangers, the bonds are tenuous, though still there.

Beneath the many-layered complexity of behavior, the woman is chained by anatomy. The male is an aggressor, at bottom. He persuades, pursues, and penetrates, even when he affects not to do so. The female recognizes, accepts and desires, his core behavior, no matter how confusing his—and her—upper layer screening may be. She wishes to be sexually attacked, though she has fears of being hurt, and doubts as to the reliability of the male she succumbs to.

As the male organ is an intruder, so is the female organ a receptor. As a man acts, so is a woman—at the procreative phase—acted upon. As a man penetrates, so is she penetrated. As the penis invades, so is the vagina invaded. A man *does,* a woman *is.* A man takes, a women is taken. A man conquers, a woman surrenders.

It is an error of the first magnitude to think that man has finally evolved out of his aggression; it is too fundamental to existence. Nor should we take the impact of the last hundred years of industrial regimentation as the final judgement of history. The meek, other-directed, male which this system seemed to mold, is already obsolete. The younger generation has junked him.

Myron Brenton has expressed the view which sums up the position of the social science community as well as the more general humanities community, and that of the feminists in particular, that to date "no one has been able to isolate an essential core peculiar to each sex, a basic something, an immutable organic quality peculiarly different in the male and female." It is this belief which provides the foundation for feminism.

I have labored to show that there *is* such an immutable, organic something, different in the male and female. The essential core of masculinity is aggression. The essential core of femininity is the lack thereof. The social scientists' and feminists' belief that the only important differences between the sexes, except reproductive ones, are culturally determined ones, is obsolete. This point of view has been overtaken by scientific research and has been found to be wanting. The behavior trait of aggression is organic. While it can be amplified or reduced by cultural indoctrination, it exists independent of culture and must be recognized as a fundamental psychological difference between the sexes.

I have offered ethological, genetic, endocrinological, anatomical, experimental-psychological, and psychoanalytical evidence for the greater aggression of the male, leading to his domination of the female. I have shown that domination and subordination have their roots in biology and are not arbitrary cultural happenings. By the time the infant is exposed to the winds of culture, the twig has already been bent. Culture simply bends it further or pushes it back a little.

But nothing that has been said here leads inevitably to the conclusion that the female is so passive as to be inert and that she must be externally energized. Nor has anything brought forward here pointed to the necessity of the feminine role being one of shallowness, immaturity, or intellectual incompetence. To be unequal, does not mean to be stunted. In the intricate dance of life, the ballerina can become a prima donna, but she will become so in cooperation with her partner.

But in utilizing the resources given to her, and exploring the limits of her potential the female must understand that there are still natural limits. There are only two modes of existence for humans, the masculine and the feminine. The male who rejects the masculine mode must be feminine. The female who rejects the feminine mode must be masculine. This means that a person must be either in a dominant or subordinate relationship to another. No intimate relationship can ever be quite neutral or quite equal.

It would therefore seem wise for cultures to continue training males to be masculine and females to be feminine. There has to be a good reason to go against the grain, and lack of equality is not a sufficiently good reason. The political theory of equality was not intended to wipe out the natural differences between the sexes. Even a severe psychosis or extreme brain damage does not wipe out a person's consciousness of his or her sex. Justice does not imply identity of function. Equality is a precept, not a percept.

Femininity is not a superstructure arbitrarily built upon a foundation of femaleness. In humans, femininity is femaleness displaced upwards. To surrender is at once a biological *and* psychological event. Even though this fusion can be dissolved— as for instance in the homosexual experience—we should not lose sight of the countless billions of times when the fusion holds. We are not being arbitrary when we give little girls dolls and little boys guns. It is not an accident that males become masculine and females feminine. It is an accident when this *doesn't* happen.

Our difficulty in understanding this arises out of the sense of incompatibility which assails us when the *fact* of inequality comes up against the *belief* in equality. But this conflict is more apparent than real. It has its origin in a too-crude statement of democratic values, rather than in a conflict of values. Democratic thought does not describe the whole of the relations between individuals, only a certain kind. To make the distinction between what types of relationships democratic theory applies to, and to what types of relationships it does not apply to, is our next task.

The Peck Order and the
Ideal of Equality

In view of the fact that aggression makes some men subordinate to others, and most women subordinate to most men, we are compelled to ask—how does the subordination of some and the domination of others square away with the democratic value of equality? Is not the fact in conflict with the value, and if the fact is true is not the value false? Does not the principle of democracy declare that the only tolerable relationship between individuals is that of equality, and does not social justice require the abolition of *sub* and *super* ordination, just as it required the abolition of slavery? The neo-feminists answer these questions affirmatively.

I should like to hazard the answer that the questions are essentially meaningless and irrelevant. There is no real conflict between the ideal of equality and the fact of subordination when each is properly understood. The fact rules in one area of human relationships, the ideal in another.

Our confusion arises from several sources. On the one hand we refuse to admit to the existence of hierarchical mechanisms deep within us, for fear that such recognition will tend to justify and perpetuate a class structure that the majority wants abolished. On the other hand, we have a very vague and imprecise idea of just what actually constitutes democratic behavior and what does not. This is a remediable weakness of education. The average person thinks of democracy in terms of the Statue of Liberty, waving the flag, and upholding motherhood. For some people it also includes the sense of being chosen by God to lead barbarians and heathens of assorted persuasions into the paths of right-eousness.

But repressing one side of a question, and allowing the other side only a most superficial statement does not lead to enlighten-ment. Not having access to an accurate statement of the problem, it is not surprising that the neo-feminists make an erroneous diagnosis of the ailment and prescribe the wrong cure.

We can start clearing up the confusion by recognizing the fact that hierarchy is the basic mode of organization among social animals. Hierarchy is energized by spacing aggression.

A hierarchy is not the same as a class structure, although the terms are analogous and to some extent overlapping. Hierarchies are ladders of status in simple societies of few numbers. Where societies swell, classes appear. Classes are dominant and subordi-nate also, but they have other elements as well. Classes have superior access to things and ideas, which results in a special power. A dominant individual is more aggressive. A dominant class, though originally composed of individuals who were more aggressive, might continue in dominance with only members of average aggression, because it continues to have superior access to the levers of power.

Though separable in thought, the hierarchy due to greater ag-gression and the hierarchy due to superior access, mingle together in reality: Some of the richest and the smartest are also the most aggressive. But in mammals beneath man on the evolutionary scale, aggression alone is the cause of hierarchy. This is especially clear among the simians. Hierarchy is quite strong among the baboon troops that live in open country, though weaker among chimpanzees still living in the forest. But it is always in evidence. Man's simian ancestor, in turn, inherited the hierarchical social organization intact from below. It is interesting to note that fourth-grade children intuitively understand hierarchy without explanation, whereas to convey the ideas of democracy to them requires some discussion.

Wherever we look, whether at baboon troops on the march, rhesus monkeys in the lab, or chimpanzees in the zoo, or whether we look at men in Stone Age societies or in our own mass indus-trial society, we find hierarchy. Two hundred years of democratic influence have modified our spontaneous hierarchy at many im-portant points, but it is still there. Lovers are unequal, and so are friends. An individual is either dominant or subordinate, or both, at different moments. The one thing he never is, is equal.

Nonetheless, there are obvious points of difference between our hierarchy and that of the baboons. In our society the strong do not hoard all the best females for themselves in harems. Many desirable women are left over for the lesser lights, and it is not at all unusual to see the least dominant male mated to a very choice female. Why should this be the case for human society and the opposite be the case for the baboons, where one dominant individual has a harem and many subordinates are bachelors?

The answer lies in man's limitations as a predator. The inefficient human predator must band together with his fellow incompetents and make up in quanity what he lacks in quality. He thus finds himself in society—which exacts a certain price. To get help he is required to share the spoils—the females as well as the meat. While his superior aggression works for his domination, his dependency upon help works against it. And the bigger the hunting party gets (or the "work" party) the less dominant he becomes. Still, the leader *never* becomes just one of the boys, because the group cannot function without a leader, and thus the hierarchy persists. Though it may be a weak one, it may also be extreme. The relationship between parent and child remains one of extreme hierarchy, despite the ever-changing fashions in child rearing.

But society does bring with it many problems, especially the problem of *size*. One rarely sees a baboon troop larger than forty or fifty members. Even the far more numerous monkeys are actually segregated into smaller groups. Even in today's mass populations individuals still live out their lives within a smaller group. The reader need only count his Christmas card list to find out how big his particular "society" really is.

Millions of years of living in small groups have programmed the human, genetically and neurologically, for small group relationships. Yet the world now has a population of over four billion, and the neighborhood a density of thousands. This is something radically different from what our genes were originally equipped to handle, and one of the signs of this may be the extraordinary incidence of aggression between humans, especially in times of war. Let us compare, briefly, the experience of living in a small band and the experience of living in a massive population.

In the band, the individual is born into a family, which merges into a clan which broadens into a tribe. He is *intimately* acquainted with his own extended family, and *familiar* with everyone else in the tribe. His nervous system, therefore, is programmed not only for small groups but for spontaneous, informal, intimate, and familiar relations.

One day a figure appears on the horizon. It walks upright, wears an apron over its genitals, has two arms, two legs, and one head—suitably decorated—and has a mouth making sounds suspiciously like language. The creature is like oneself—it is a man—yet it is different. One needs a new word to describe this phenomenon, this combination of the known and unknown. This creature is strange. This human being is a *stranger*.

Something new has been added to the human experience, something the human nervous system had to invent an entirely new response for. A new dimension of experience has opened up. The species now recognizes, not only a distinction between humans and other animals, but a distinction between kinds of human beings—familiar ones and strange ones, known and unknown ones.

One of the characteristics that make the stranger strange is that he is an outsider, a nonmember of the tribe. This fact requires a new way of relating to him, and a new way is therefore invented: Relations with this stranger are *formal*.

If our way of relating to him is different from our interaction with people inside the tribe, and our relationship to him is formal, then our relationships with people inside the tribe must always have been something else. They were. They were *informal*.

The intrusion of the stranger into the midst of the tribe forced our kind to think about matters they had previously taken for granted. The stimulus made explicit that which had always been implicit. There had always been rules of conduct, but they had been intuitively understood. Now that they had become explicit, they had to be reasoned out accurately. The rules thus became "laws."

There is no end to the novelties that followed in the stranger's wake. He was neither a father, brother, cousin, nor clansman. He did not fit into the hierarchy. We could neither dominate him, nor subordinate ourselves to him. More hard thought was required, and another new concept was created: The stranger was an "equal."

Thus, this stranger, when he appeared on the horizon, was the bearer of a revolution. His mere presence caused man to coin new words and articulate new concepts. His visit to the tribe was the first elemental experience which later in history led to the formulation of democratic ideas. The formal, explicit, legal, equalitarian, relationships that exist between strangers, are the relationships of democracy. Conversely, informal, implicit rules that exist between intimates are the relationships of hierarchy.

This concept of the stranger, which I at first used only as a shorthand metaphor, turns out to have objective reality. Its significance has already been detected in two different worlds, the anthropological, and the psychological. The anthropologist Peter Farb points out that the primitive mind is obsessed with kinship problems:

> "If a stranger arrives in another band's territory, he is usually greeted with elaborate politeness while he sits on the outskirts of the camp and talks with the old men about possible family relationships. If the stranger can trace any kind of relationship to someone in the band, then he is accepted into it; it is known just where he fits into the society and how to behave towards him. Otherwise he would represent a danger. The old men might chase him away or simply kill him—for he would be similar in status to a madman in our society." (6)

Aaron Esman, the psychoanalyst, in his turn points to the well known psychological phenomenon of *xenophobia,* which is the fear of the stranger. It is a rather common human ailment. (7)

We must ask why the two modes—the mode of the stranger and the mode of the familiar—come into conflict, with the mode of the stranger tending to push the other out. This happens mostly because one day the stranger ceases to be a transient outsider. Because the two modes are different, the individual is faced with two different directives of behavior in any given situation. He can follow either one, but not both.

A day comes when the tribe swells to such proportions that it is now composed of strangers rather than familiars. The stranger who was once an outsider and a minority, is now an insider and a majority. He who was once a temporary problem of protocol, has become a permanent stress factor. Life becomes transformed and consciousness becomes dominated, not by the informal, spontaneous, rules of familiars, but by the formal, deliberate rules of strangers. Society is transformed from a comfortable, informal, hierarchy into a cold, formal system, based upon rules of behavior and principles of justice. Within the home one still lives in the old hierarchy, but outside of it is a world of laws which enjoin a different kind of behavior. And the center of gravity has shifted to the outside.

What is more, economic changes have taken place along with

the social ones. Our kind no longer has direct access to the food supply, or depends for it upon intimates. Instead, we have become dependent upon strangers for access to it. Most of these strangers don't care in the least whether we survive or not, therefore our relationship to the stranger has now become a crucial one. If we fail to handle it properly we can be cut off from the food supply and starve in the midst of plenty. Unfortunately, despite our efforts to handle it well, we frequently botch the job because we were programmed for a small-scale world of friends, not a big world of strangers. And the severance of our umbilical cord makes us insecure, which stimulates our aggression. In time, over many centuries, it dawns upon us that we are not living in a world we are equipped for. We are out of joint with it, ill-adapted, or "sick." We are in a condition of permanent malaise.

We have two clear choices: We must either adapt ourselves to this world, or we must adapt it to ourselves. The latter possibility seems staggering, so we try the former. But it doesn't work. As adaptable as we appear to be, we cannot become comfortable in this new world. Ever so slowly we come to the realization that we must, after all, undertake the gigantic task of adapting it to us.

The domination of society by strangers implies the domination of society by equality. But, during the period of the first mass societies, the very reverse holds true. In the valley of the Nile and of the Tigris-Euphrates rivers, the hierarchy swells to enormous proportions. Pharaohs, priests, generals, and scribes lord it over the mass of mankind. The implicit hierarchy of early man was dwarfed by the explicit hierarchy of mass society. What happened to equality? How do we explain its glaring absence?

We explain it by time. The time available since the development of mass societies has not yet been sufficient for organizing principles to work themselves out. In the four or five thousand years that evolution has been at work, the principles of democracy have been transforming society. But they have not yet completed the task. There have been complications, the principal one being economic. Scarcity cannot support a democratic society, which demands plenty. Thus, scarcity of things and ideas spawns a class structure, and this class structure operates as a brake on the working out of democratic principles.

But enough time has now elapsed to show that mass society is being inexorably democratized, though more slowly than many would wish. The idea of the fundamental equality of persons in social relationships is at the bottom of the Code of Hammurabi, and becomes even more visible in the later Roman law. It receives its first explicit formulation, in religious terms, in the teaching of Jesus that all men are brothers, which is simply a religious way of saying that all men are equal.

The time needed to work out the principle of social equality was further extended by the collapse of the Roman Empire. The evolution that had started in the first mass societies of Egypt and Mesopotamia, continued in the maritime societies of the Mediterranean and Greece, had gathered momentum by the time Rome got into the act, and was changing things rapidly. But when Rome fell, this inner dynamic came to a halt, resulting in regression to a lower level of vitality. For a thousand years society reverted to small-group living. It was not until the time of the Renaissance that things got moving again, and not until the time of the American and French revolutions that democratic principles were installed as guiding beliefs. More generations are required to translate the principles into realities.

Once more there came an interruption, this time in the shape of the Industrial Revolution. The early stages, at least, of technical development require the organization of people into disciplined armies of production. But the armies of production are as rigidly hierarchical as the armies of war. So, while in the political sector of life evolution is going forward in the direction of greater democracy, in the economic sector we regress to rigid hierarchies. Before the economic sector ceases to be an obstacle to the further democratization of society it must reach a stage where it can produce plenty—without discipline. (This may or may not already have happened, at least in the United States, shortly after World War II.) The economic sector of society must pass over this threshold before it ceases to be an obstacle to the ultimate organization of society in accordance with the principles first suggested by the entry of that the single stranger into the tribe.

Meanwhile, the worldwide effect of democratic theory on political and social organization—in the public sphere of life—is too obvious to require further elaboration. Our time is one of constant revolution due the effect of these ideas on old institutions. Everywhere, democratic ideas have made serious modifications in the hierarchy.

Among public school students, for example, hierarchies still form, but no longer on the basis of parental status. The basis now is one of individual charisma, or good looks, or athletic skill, on anything but the parents' power position. The poor working-class boy of personal force becomes class president and the setter of standards. The descendant of the *Mayflower* with no personal merit drifts to the margins of the school world. The theatrical world is full of successes from the lowest walks of life. While such examples are part of the folklore of capitalism, they are also true to life. Every one of them is a proof that democratic ideals are gradually becoming the organizing principles of mass society— no matter how absurd that may sound to those currently not making out, and with little prospect of doing so. It is the mode of the stranger, not the mode of the friend, that is humanizing society in the long run, because it is to the abstract ideals of social justice that those on the bottom look for relief, not to their familiars or relatives.

I have sketched this process of hierarchy modification to demonstrate the effect of democratic ideals of the mode of the stranger on the old hierarchy based on aggression alone.

In the world of the friendly and the familiar, democratic principles have no place. In this world, the hierarchy stemming from spacing aggression rules—limited, of course, by the legal rights necessary to protect the individual from an excess of friendly tyranny. In this world, the stronger rule the weaker, but usually with love and consideration. The man rules the woman and the parent rules the child. Democracy stops at the door of the home, the fraternal lodge, and the parked car in which lovers are ensconced.

It is in the world of the stranger—where the woman is comparatively free from sexual aggression, and where spacing aggression will eventually be at its weakest—that democratic principles apply. Strangers have signed a nonaggression pact, and have repudiated aggression as a social organizing principle.

It is here that women can look for growth, change, and a rough approximation of equality. But if women do not dwell in this world of the stranger, they can hardly expect to share in its benefits.

It was the substance of the first feminist revolt to get women out of the home and into this world, where growth would not be stifled. By and large, that movement was successful in terms of knocking down obstacles and winning a parity of right. But it was not successful in winning women a parity of power because they did not stay in that world. They must return to it and stay in it, if they are to overcome and resolve their crisis. But while they do so they should definitely be aware that even here, there is still a force working against a perfectly just, perfectly equal relationship.

The constant receptivity of the human female to the sexual advances of the male makes for a powerful substratum of sexuality in human life, for which there is no equivalent in other species. Even without the aid of advertisers saturating the media with eroticism, there would still be an undertow of immense power. This undertow acts as a drag on the female's search for equality in the outside world. Sexuality has a way of turning equal strangers into unequal friends. The minute coworkers go out on a date they cease being equals. The more sexual the female, the more energy she puts into eroticism, either in search or avoidance, and the less energy she has for other types of relationships.

This eroticism is a tidal force making for male dominance and it does not disappear in the formal world; it merely goes underground. Even where the female is happily mated or past the age of magnetizing males, the habits of a lifetime linger on. Contact with men is still pleasureable for its own sake, and the mind of the older woman is still young.

Adding to the undermining pull of eroticism are the other two limiting forces working against the achievement of a theoretically "neat" equality.

The average woman, being less aggressive than the average man, is therefore handicapped. In the science-fiction future, when we program our own genes, the woman who really wants to compete will probably be able to call for an extra dose of aggression to be added to her chromosome packet.

The second limiting force can be cured in a much shorter time. The biggest obstacle to the already aggressive female is the fact that she is usually in the wrong place at the right time. When everyone else is at the starting gate, she is likely to be in the maternity ward. By the time she returns to the starting gate, the race is over and the important prizes have been distributed. Her male competitors gave the race everything they had. She gave it half her energy.

Of course this could be easily be cured by postponing children until after thirty, rather than having them so close to twenty. By that time the woman would be both economically and emotionally mature, and the benefits to the child and society of having children born to stable parents *only*, would be incalculable. Lack of disciplined thinking has caused women to blunder badly in the matter of timing childbirth. They have been told that they are most efficient at having babies near age twenty, and they have taken this to mean that they are *inefficient* later on, rather than *less* efficient. But a woman in her third decade is just as capable of bearing children as she has to be, and she is a much better mother. As a result, the modern American girl has created an obstacle to her own development that need not be there at all. Possibly, of course, this muddled thinking is not the result of a lack of mental discipline at all, but just the opposite. The eagerness to marry early and spawn right away is the device the female cop-out may be using to insure her role as perpetual dependent. Once the baby is there, it no longer matters what the male thinks. He's nailed.

If this is the case, in the future the breeder-type female may be denied her cop-out. It will not be long before woman can have her baby at any time, without interference in her working career. She will be able to have that baby in an artificial womb and have it nursed by mechanical mothers. There will be no excuse for her not to have her baby *and* work at the same time.

However, until that time, between the sabotaging pull of eroticism, the lesser aggressive endowment, and maternity duties, it would seem impossible for women to achieve a theoretically fair equality in the world of the stranger. Women, being eminently practical creatures, may be satisfied with "practical" equality. But even that will be denied her if she continues seeking equality in the place where it is not—in the home. To get it, she must go where it is—in the outer world of the stranger.

Today's woman is suspended between two worlds and is not thoroughly comfortable in either. She prefers the world of the familiar, but this world has shrunk around her, leaving her exposed. She is too big to live in its reduced dimensions, and too timid to plunge forward into a larger context. She tried it once and found it nerve-racking. In the words of Erich Fromm, she "escaped from freedom." She exists in crisis, and out of this crisis arises her demand for equality. But until she proves herself willing to pay the price of equality by an acceptance of equivalent responsibilities, her demands cannot be taken at face value. Instead, we must regard her demands as symptomatic of a deeper malady. Let us inquire more fully into its nature.

At this juncture we are turning our attention away from the general condition of man and woman, to the particular state we find them in at this historical moment. Up to this point we have heard of little but male dominion and female subordination. The emphasis was necessary to study the power relationship between the sexes. But it might appear that the new masculinist, like the old, believed in raising men by lowering women.

Far from it. The new masculinist accepts as a basic principle the right of all human beings to grow without hindrance. He does not believe in structural inequality for some as a subsidy for the superequality of others, any more than he believes in a slave class as a basis for an aristocracy. But he does not see that because the colonel is subordinate to the general in the hierarchy, he is the victim of injustice.

Nor does the neo-masculinist maintain solidarity with his brethren of all persuasions, simply for the sake of presenting a united front to the neo-feminists. There is still a remnant of the male sex that would chain women to the kitchen stove for the sake of masculine domination. The neo-masculinist dissociates himself from this position. He would not be a party to a kidnaping or enslavement. He would not force a strong woman to be subordinate to a weak man. It is up to the individual man to win and hold his woman, just as it is up to her to win and hold her man. In general, the neo-masculinist wants women to grow as far and as fast as they can, for purely selfish reasons, as well as because it is right.

But he perceives that there is a difference in initiative, toughness, and aggressiveness between men and women, just as common sense always taught. It was the expertise of the social sciences that persuaded us to ignore the evidence of our senses and accept the proposition that there were no inherent differences between the sexes. We now know that the differences in aggressive endowment dictate different status in the hierarchy. What we do not know as yet is how wide a gap there really is. We cannot adequately assess that factor until women have joined men in the world of affairs for a sufficiently long time to give us a true basis for comparison.

We must now turn our attention away from the domination-subordination axis, which is a dead end for feminine evolution, and give our undivided attention to the independence-dependence axis, which is the true direction of further feminine development. Female dependency is a matter of social values, not biology, and can be altered at will.

Unlike the concept of equality, the concept of independence receives little direct support from the biological sciences. This concept is connected more to maturity than it is to anything else, and maturity is at present a captive of the psychological and sociological sciences. Therefore, we are leaving the realm of nature for the realm of human personality and social life. Where before we were concerned mostly with *species* we are now shifting out attention to *people*.

PART II

THE PROMISING POSSIBILITIES OF INDEPENDENCE

The Feminine Option
— To Work or Wive

The fact that I have discarded lack of equality as a suitable diagnosis of the present feminine condition, does not mean that I have discarded the fact of a feminine crisis. The modern female is indeed in a crisis that needs attending to; but her symptoms cannot be relieved by false diagnosis and irrelevant therapy. I now offer as a substitute for the overworked cliché of lack of equality the concept of *lack of independence,* as a more suitable rubric for thought and a more utilitarian guide for action.

In the eyes of many feminist leaders this distinction is a semantic quibble; but this is only an indication of how far from adequate is their grasp of the problem. The two concepts lead in different directions. If one believes lack of equality to be the sickness, the remedy is propaganda and agitation—exactly what the feminist leadership is doing. But if one diagnoses lack of independence as the sickness, then something entirely different is indicated: going out and getting a job. It is the burden of the second part of this book to explore this line of thought in some detail.

A further advantage of this line of inquiry is that it coincidentally highlights the current masculine condition as well. It is impossible to consider excessive feminine dependence without simultaneously facing up to the historically unusuaul burdens being borne by the modern male. Thus we are taken out of the fragmentary contemplation of the rights of one group, and take a panoramic view of the total emotional economy. We are considering the rights and responsibilities of all.

Let us begin by plumbing the depths of the Feminine Option—to work or wive.

If it is true that the female is in another historical crisis caused by the shrinkage of her traditional world, we can reasonably expect to see some signs of this, other than her symptomatic cries for equality. The signs are there but they are scattered, and unlikely to be put into a coherent pattern except by professional pattern arrangers. The average person is not likely to pay much attention to them.

Let us start arbitrarily, with the observation that American soldiers, when sent abroad to occupy or fight, show a decided prejudice in favor of the women they encounter, a prejudice that cannot be written off as a result of the proximity of hotblooded youth to receptive young females. During World War II, in England, France, Germany, Italy, the Philippines, and Japan, American men found something they didn't have at home. They found it again in Korea. Wherever and whenever the Coca-Cola girl has been matched up against foreign competition, the Coca-Cola boy has voted her a loser. Given the fact that the boys were meeting these foreign girls at the very time when they would have been selecting brides at home, the elders of our tribe were able to write off the phenomenon as an unfortunate by-product of war. But the girls who lost out, having been reared on a belief in their own superior beauty and attractiveness, found the development disturbing. Most people did not connect the phenomenon to any others, and in time forgot about it.

Let *us* connect it with another apparently random phenomenon.

Many social observers have noted that the European woman, by and large, does not like the American woman. She *does* like the American man. European men, on the average, like neither American sex.

Both European sexes are united in regarding American women as hard, selfish, and domineering, with an exploitative attitude towards men. But the European woman is inclined to feel sympathy towards the American male because of this, while the European man responds with contempt for the American male's apparent spinelessness in permitting it.

Let us now connect the American soldiers' preference for foreign women, and the European negative opinion of the American woman, to the fact that European observers have not been making their criticisms of the American character just in this century, since we began sending loads of rich tourists abroad. First-rate, original minds have been making the same kinds of comment ever since the early 1800's. (1)

Now, I think, we have sufficient smoke to suspect a fire. Let us inspect what the neo-feminists have to say on the subject. Simone de Beauvoir, presumably basing her opinions on her observations of European women, uses such words as "frivolous," "infantile," and "irresponsible," in describing her own sex. But we cannot use these descriptions as applying to American women.

However, Betty Friedan, after a lifetime of observing the American female, goes even further. Though she never offers us a definition of femininity, there can be little doubt as to her evaluation of it. A "weak ego or sense of self," "a weak superego or human conscience," are some of her descriptions. Others include, "a renunciation of active aims, ambitions, or interests of one's own to live through others"; "incapacity for abstract thought"; and "retreat from activity directed outward . . . in favor of activity directed inward, or fantasy."

One gets the distinct impression that both feminists are reluctant to give uninhibited descriptions of their sisters, for fear of alienating the audience they wish to influence. Reading between the lines, it appears obvious that both Friedan and de Beauvoir regard their own sex as seriously deficient in several desirable attributes, and that Friedan sees the American woman as in a more serious situation than the European. If this is the case, and I believe it is, then modern American femininity has had something added to it which was not put there by biology. Furthermore, none of these attributes are necessary aspects of femininity. One need not be infantile, irresponsible, weak, scatterbrained, or a dweller in fantasy, to be a feminine female. Yet these traits are accepted as a necessary part of femininity by masses of women as well as men. Psychotherapists pinpoint these traits as indicative of "disorientation."

Add to this the fact that female suicide, alcoholism, narcotic addiction, and just plain crime, are on a rampant increase, and one begins to feel that a stronger term than "disoriented" may be in order. The term *neurosis* seems eminently appropriate; for what we are dealing with here are signs of arrested emotional development rather than signs of femininity. Nature has decreed no inevitable conflict between femininity and maturity.

Betty Friedan recognizes the condition full well, without naming it, when she says, "It is my thesis that the core of the problem for women today is . . . a stunting or evasion of growth, perpetuated by the feminine mystique."

She goes on to quote a study which proves that many college girls show no growth at all during their college experience, using their devotion to future motherhood as an excuse for avoiding the intellectual guts of college life. Many of the girls know that this is not the real reason they avoid intellectual growth, and feel the need to rationalize. The rationalization is, of course, the old standby: they do not wish to be "brainy" for fear of losing out in the marriage competition. Apart from the fact that they are equating femininity with stupidity—which their I. Q.'s belie—school counsellors get the distinct impression that "interest in men and marriage is a kind of defense mechanism against intellectual development." That is, motherhood is a convenient excuse for avoiding responsible contact with the world.

But whereas brainless euphoria has been consciously sought by the middle class college girl, the working class girl exists in that state without effort. She tends to be unaware of the fact that to be a female is not the same as to be a vegetable. She has yet to find out that the head has potential functions besides holding up a hairdo.

We must look beyond the fear of spinsterhood for the reason why working class girls are strangers to cogitation, and middle class girls deliberately avoid it. Anti-intellectual men cannot be made responsible for this flight from intelligence and maturity, because such men have become a minority. Nor can lack of aggression account for more than a small part.

I have already given a superficial reason: Women found the world of work a dissatisfying illusion, and came to the conclusion that if frustration is unavoidable, one can be more comfortably frustrated over a cup of coffee in the kitchen than a cup of coffee in an office. This was where the feminist movement bogged down. Few women relished the strains that accompanied the independence they sought.

But now is the time to dig beneath superficial answers. Why has the work experience affected women so adversely? Why did they react to it so differently from men? The answer is simple.

Women don't *have* to work—men do. They react to work differently from men because they have an alternative open to them that men do not have. They have the option *not* to work.

We react to this option as though it were the most natural thing in the world, when in fact it is most extraordinary. This option is entirely new in history. It is a pervasive social characteristic only of modern times, and only of advanced industrial societies. Women never had this option before, either in the western world or in primitive tribes. Always before they had been compelled to work just like men, in addition to having babies.

This fact, that women have acquired a choice as to whether to work or not to work is at the root of their present crisis. Nature does not tolerate a static state or indecision in organic systems. Organisms either grow or decay, but never stand still. To suffer indecision, to appear to be standing still, is to be in a slow, downward spiral of decay, to be deteriorating. It might also be compared to being 'frozen' in a neurotic attitude. This posture is currently the pervasive characteristic of an entire sex; we may well characterize that sex as being in a state of crisis.

However, if women were simply compelled to work as men are, there would be no peculiarly feminine crisis. There would continue to be a series of crises, of course, but no single one attributable solely to being a female. It is my thesis that the mere existence of such an option in the life of a female, the very fact that she may exercise it when she so desires, and repudiate it when the going gets rough, has now become the central molding factor in feminine life. Her position is that of a soldier at the front who can walk away from the battle any time he wants to. That is why "the Option," which we now capitalize, has proved a vitiating source of paralysis to her, instead of a source of life enrichment. She does not have sufficient aggression to stick to the grind, without compulsion. The man has no choice but to hold fast under fire or be shot for desertion. The mere existence of the Option, therefore, is sufficient cause for widespread feminine arrested development. When the battle gets too rough, she can always retreat into marriage. (Conversely, the very knowledge that this retreat is open to her, is what gives the female who does choose to compete her sense of confidence.) Therefore, in order to insure that women not throw away their chance at growth and maturity, they will have to be denied the chance to cop-out.

If there is one thing that persistently makes men in authority unwilling to promote women to responsible jobs, it is the knowledge—hotly denied by feminists but repeatedly verified by experience—that they frequently lose their commitment to their careers, always with a first-class cover story.

Women of ambition like to think that they, personally, can be counted on. But men in a position to see the opposite happen *do* see it happen, and all too often to run the risk of relying on the next woman's word. The man *knows* he can rely on a male; he is taking a chance on a woman. He also knows that despite her best intentions she may have an "accident," or a disgruntled husband may sabotage her career by a well timed impregnation, or by transfer to another part of the country.

Every faculty member of a college or graduate school can testify to the high rate of attrition among devoted "career" women. The minute the pressure is on, they start dropping out for marriage. Professors in a position to dispense patronage know that giving a scarce grant to a woman is like throwing it away. And even if she gets the coveted Ph. D., she will rarely be in a position to produce that research which justifies the money spent. One need only to compare the vows and convictions of career-bent freshmen and sophomore college girls with their actions during senior year, to realize that desertion is wholesale at every level of decision. The minute other girls start getting married, the would-be career girl gets cold feet and panics. The same thing is observed by personnel men in industry.

The tacit understanding of the existence of the Option in the life of a woman, though rarely articulated, is central to the differentiation of the sexes. The little boy learns that when he grows up he *must* work. The little girl experiences no such imperative.

For the boy, the foreknowledge that he must earn a living through work well done, is roughly equivalent to knowing that he must face life. But for the little girl there is no *must*. She can dally, fantasize, and equivocate. She can therefore avoid the foreknowledge that she will have to face life.

Consequently, even when she does choose to work, the work does not have the same significance for her as for the male. If she fails to work well, she is only a poor worker, not a flunking female. But a man who fails to hold down his job is not just a poor worker, he is a failing male.

It is woman's total failure to grasp this point which also accounts for her failure to understand male resentment at equal pay for equal work. Her work may be equal, but her responsibilities are not. The man feels he should get more for his greater responsibility, or else should have no more responsibility than the woman. She feels it is unjust for her to get less for the same kind of work, which would be true only if her responsibilities were the same as his. But she doesn't know about that. She has taken her protected status for granted and does not wish to pay for it with lesser privilege.

It is apparent to most men, but to very few feminists, that, standing side by side in a factory, doing precisely the same work at the same pay, the male and female are still living in two different worlds. His work is a matter of both physical and psychological survival. Hers is not. However reluctant young men may be to enter the world of work, ultimately they accept work as a validation of their masculinity, as well as for the pay check. To bring home the bacon is a hunter's qualification for life. To do work that is bitterly resented, is only that much more testimony to a man's manhood. He can take whatever is dished out. He can survive.

Work, to women, insofar as it has any symbolic value at all, is mostly a monument to injustice or wretched fate. Either the man who should be supporting her has not yet arrived on the scene, or he is failing to perform his task in life properly. It is because women have rejected work and, through work, the responsibility for their own survival, that they live in a state of general neurosis.

Man, forced to face life by being forced to work, lives on a growth curve and gets stronger, even when the job is stultifying and stunts his growth in other dimensions of experience. Basically, he is still in contact with reality. He may have a cold but he is not suffering from pneumonia.

In rejecting the legitimacy of work and responsibility for herself, and demanding dependency, woman has put herself on the critical list—though she may not even be aware of her illness. Given the anomie of the work world at this phase of history, she has a strong incentive to rationalize her attitude as a normal and natural one, one that has always been and will always continue to be. She has some support for seeing herself as a perpetual dependent with no responsibilities in life beyond childbearing, even though this is a serious misreading of the historical record. The neurotic is comfortable in his neurosis, the homosexual comfortable in his homosexuality, and even the prisoner gets used to his chains. It will take more than persuasion to get women back on a growth curve.

Especially is this true when the future outlook opens up the possibility of even greater neurosis and a more dangerous avoidance of reality than the present allows. Overpopulation, radical change in maternal practices, and the incipient arrival of the science-fiction future, make the Option wider, and hence more threatening.

In the near future, overpopulation may make a maximum limit of two children per couple mandatory, which will considerably reduce the time a woman may spend in maternity-related activity. The new standards already encourage having only one child; and the decision to have no children at all is rapidly becoming perfectly acceptable.

Furthermore, a reaction has set in against the overintense child-raising practices prevalent during the forties and fifties. In the future, mothers will spend less time, rather than more, with the fewer children they are going to have, and the home will shrink even more as a life context for women.

According to Philip Slater, chairman of the Department of Sociology at Brandeis University, Dr. Spock tended to "encourage Pygmalianesque fantasies in mothers." Every child is not a Bach or Beethoven, and when one of these geniuses does come along the average mother simply does not have the training or talent to bring this genius out. Hence, her complete domesticity is wasted. The childraising role has been magnified into a full-time job, which it is not. In all other societies and during all previous periods of history women have performed a variety of other tasks concomitantly with raising their children. The idea of devoting their entire lives to this one task never occurred to earlier generations of women. Thus, on the basis of short-range considerations alone, woman can no longer view her domestic role as her all.

The long-run considerations are even more devastating. Never before has woman had to face the actual obsolescence of her prime biological task, the conceiving and raising of children. She must face it now. The neo-feminists have advised men to adjust to the revolutionary fact that muscle has been superseded by machines. It is now time for men to return the compliment and advise women to accept the fact that soon their services may no longer be needed to reproduce the species! When this comes to pass, their last shred of justification for lifelong dependency will disappear. There is a kind of cruel poetic justice in the fact that women will be faced with a brand of "equality" they had not anticipated—the equality of uselessness, of enforced "retirement." It will be interesting to note whether they can keep their cool in the face of it.

We had our first hint of the coming dispensation some years ago when it was discovered that a "mechanical" mother had been accepted by newborn monkeys. The substitute was made out of a few cents' worth of terrycloth and wire. Upon being presented with this soft item resembling a mother's bosom, the monkeys accepted it as the real thing, and thereafter responded to it as to a mother. They grew up unimpaired in any way. While human infants grow up to be much smarter than monkeys, at birth they are not; and the experiment demonstrated that it was theoretically possible to substitute mechanical mothers for real ones.

This provocative lead was not pounced upon by industry and used as a starting point for the construction of baby-sitting machines; but other developments have shown that the mechanical mother may be among the easier things to be created on the road to making the female reproductively obsolete.

She has already been obsolete for decades as a source of mother's milk. Most babies today are bottle babies; but this development took place so long ago that it was never connected to the scientific revolution, and was never seen as an augury of the coming obsolescence of the mother herself. It was not anywhere nearly so dramatic, for example, as the discovery of artificial insemination. This development, connected as it was to the replacement of male muscle by machines, was seen as one more significant step in the dethronement of the male.

But now it seems that the mother herself is on the way out. A significant step in this direction was the discovery of superovulation. In this process, the human female is stimulated to lay several eggs at once, instead of the normal one. These eggs can be stored in banks, like sperm, giving our scientific wizards the essentials to begin experimenting with test-tube maternity. One development follows hard on another these days, and human eggs have already been successfully fertilized in a test tube.

The next step will be to transplant the fertilized egg into the womb of a woman other than the mother of the egg. Artificial wombs have not yet been developed that will incubate the human egg; but current experiments with artificial wombs have already kept lamb's eggs alive for fifty-five hours.

Using the eggs of lower mammals, our scientists have already been able to fertilize frog eggs artificially and to grow them to maturity in the laboratory. They have even gone so far as to replicate frogs, making one exactly like another, by transplanting body cells rather than germ cells, into the egg of a frog as nuclei. This is no more and no less than virgin birth! The only drawback is that only females can be replicated. As no male sperm is involved in fertilizing the egg, there are no Y chromosomes to make males and the offspring of the replicates must be female only. Still, virgin birth is virgin birth.

Among other feats of wizardry performed in the laboratory have been the following: the fusion of the cells of two different species, sheep and goats, from which a nucleus was obtained with the hereditary qualities of both; the nucleus of one type of creature has been injected into the egg of another type, with the egg developing the characteristics of the nucleus; and the fertilization of mice eggs in a test tube followed by their successful transplantation into the womb of another female, there successfully growing into a fetus. According to Dr. David Whittington, who performed the experiment, there is no practical difference between a mouse egg and a human egg.

On the horizon we see the possibility of controlling the sex of a child; children being born to geographically separated parents; children being born of parents who are dead; women giving birth to other women's children; test tube births requiring neither male nor female donorship, etc.

Exciting as these developments are, we must put them to one side and consider their human implications. There will be little left to the female claim to dependency upon the male, when she is no longer necessarily incapacitated by childbirth or childbearing. This kind of obsolescence is likely to be more psychologically devastating to the female than the introduction of machinery and artificial insemination was to the male. When babies are being born in test tubes, someone will still have to watch the test tubes; but if the neo-feminists insist that man abdicate his dominant position now, because his muscle is obsolete, will they not be hoist on their own petard later? What will this unemployed mother be doing while he is still flexing his atrophied muscles? It would be wise for women to prepare for the inevitable future now, by refraining from making demands of adjustment on men that they themselves will not want to meet when the shoe is on the other foot. Between the existing obsolescence of the house-wife, and the coming obsolescence of the mother, woman will have nowhere to go but *out,* into the world. Yet she will enter it with the same emotional equipment she has carried for millions of years, and will find there something less than complete equality.

The crisis in feminine life, then, will get worse before it gets better. Its source is not inequality, but the Option that has opened up to women, which has created a paralysis of will, afflicting almost the whole female sex. Very few individuals escape it. The majority of women live in a state of neurosis which, being so wide-spread, has gone undetected, and has masqueraded as femininity. Its principal feature, dependency, is seen as a feature of normalcy because it is so pervasive, rather than as the symptom of malaise which it really is. And, as is characteristic of neurosis, defense mechanisms are created to protect the symptom. Women persist in regarding dependency as a condition thrust upon them by the authoritarian male, rather than as a condition which they themselves help to create. By regarding dependency as a right they are biologically entitled to, the female has institutionalized her abnormality as normality.

Woman was precipitated into this condition of total dependency by the Industrial Revolution. Her initial response to her crisis was healthy. She knocked down the obstacles to recovery, wrote a prescription for cure through work and independence, and then welshed on taking the medicine she herself had prescribed. Her crisis, then, is one of doubt and delay, not lack of equality. When she takes her medicine at last, she will be cured. When she makes certain that her daughter has taken it, she will have overcome the historical crisis.

Though the average woman will intuitively understand and accept my statement as the significance of the Option, she will resist mightily my claim that in recoiling from the necessity to immerse herself in the cold water of the economic world, she threw herself into an exaggerated dependency on the male. To the female of our time, this is not only heresy but stupidity. Has not woman always been dependent upon man? Is this not the nature of *homo sapiens*—for men to go out and bring in the bacon and for women to cook it?

A succinct answer to this question is—*no*. This belief is one of the most massive errors in history.

It is true that since time immemorial women have been subordinate to men; but it is not true that they were also totally dependent. That is a refinement of modern times, specifically of the last hundred years. Here is an instance where the use of the terms inferior-superior has resulted in near-catastrophic error and the intuition of feminine subordination has been confused with the concept of dependency.

The reverse of this proposition is much nearer the truth. Modern feminine total dependency has had a very short career, historically speaking. It has been an unfortunate fact of life only since the beginning of the Industrial Revolution, and it was only an idiosyncrasy of American life that exacerbated the fact. While industrialization everywhere caused a crisis in the male-female relationship, nowhere else did this crisis approach institutionalized parasitism as closely as in the United States. Let us deal with these developments in the order of their importance: first, the general impact of industrialization on the power relation between the sexes, and secondly, the effect which American culture has had on making a bad thing worse.

Recall that the simian female, an herbivorous creature, is subordinate to the male but not a dependent. She is easily capable of feeding herself and her offspring. However, when the hominid type went over to predation and became a meateater, the hominid female did not become a hunter and became dependent upon the male for meat as her source of protein. But this dependency was of a radically different nature than the total female dependence of advanced civilization.

This first stage of life, the hunting stage, was, precisely speaking, a hunting and gathering stage, in which the men specialized in securing meat and the women specialized in securing vegetable foods. It was an economic partnership, not a total dependency. The female was dependent for meat only, and she paid for this meat by supplying other foods. Thus, each was dependent upon the other. The man did not experience the woman as a liability or responsibility as he did the child, but as a coworker and asset of subordinate rank.

Throughout all the changes and vicissitudes of subsequent history, this relationship never basically changed for most people. In fact, it was probably the economic discoveries of women that caused the first great transformation. As gatherers, it is most likely that women were the first to make observations which eventually led to settled agriculture. And it was agriculture, in turn, which dwarfed hunting as a source of food.

With the advent of settled farm life the woman's economic importance leaped spectacularly higher. A farm is no more and no less than a household industry, and this sort of family economy characterized family life right up until the Industrial Revolution. In this type of economic unit the female is crucial. In no sense can the man be said to be supporting woman, as he does today; each was an essential part of the productive machinery. When we look back we still have the illusion of female dependency because the man was still dominant. But this was only an illusion, and the female was, by and large, not a dependent, merely a subordinate. A farmer who lost his wife lost more than a love object. He lost an economic partner who had to be replaced quickly because the economic unit could not function without her.

In the long hunting and gathering stage that preceeded the household industry, the fact that the man left the hearth to hunt, seems to parallel the fact that he goes out to work today. But the parallel breaks down when we note that the primeval woman did her gathering while he was away while the modern housewife merely cooks and cleans. The cavewoman did that *plus*.

As civilization grew in complexity and specialization of labor emerged, some men followed trades, and the woman's role kept pace. While the man blacksmithed, the woman took over the farming chores completely. If he became a full-time blacksmith or shoemaker and the family gave up farming, she became a sales clerk, bookkeeper, and supervisor of apprentices, as well as the homemaker. Here still, the man did not experience the woman as a childlike dependent but as an economic asset.

Even in the lofty castles of the later feudal age the aristocratic lady was a worker of significance. Anyone who has read the household account books of a medieval castle or Renaissance manor is staggered by the magnitude of the task it was to keep one running. Many of these women who come down to us in legend as ladies of leisure were in fact running a business with fifty to a hundred employees!

In many primitive tribes a woman must be bought and paid for, because her father regards her not as a total dependent but rather as an economic asset. He will not let her go without compensation.

When, then, did the man come to experience the woman as a total, childlike, dependent? It was at the time when the Industrial Revolution broke down the family industry, took work out of the home and put it in a building called a factory. Men went with it, and women stayed behind. Work was now a thing apart, and became the central experience of life for men. Home and hearth became secondary.

Though the woman had remained behind in the hunt too, this time her remaining behind was drastically different: now she stopped being a producer of food or money, and thus ceased to carry significant responsibility. Naturally her power and influence atrophied.

It was at this point in history that men and women began having fundamentally different life experiences, apart from the differences caused by sexuality; and it was at this point that men began experiencing women as total dependents as well as subordinates.

The woman remained poised at that moment of history, while the man has passed beyond it. The woman did not then and has not now, passed over the threshold of the world of the familiar into the world of the stranger. Even though many women were driven out of the home and into factory slavery, psychologically they still remained in the world of the home. But home and shop are not simply places, they are also modes of experiencing life. The female is now twice removed from the male—once by the hierarchy of subordination in the home and again by experiencing life in the mode of the familiar, while man experiences it mostly in the world of the strange.

This difference in the fundamental mode of experiencing life is the crucial source of the psychic disequilibrium in the emotional economy. It will not be rectified until such time as women join men in the psychological world of the stranger. For not only does man experience life in a different mode from the woman, but he experiences the woman herself as an outsider—as a dependent-subordinate instead of as a subordinate coworker. This extraordinary state of affairs, far from being an eternal one, has crept up on us gradually, and has only been going on for a few decades. It is an abnormal state of affairs, and we have been taking the abnormal as the norm.

At the time of the Industrial Revolution the woman still had enormous loads of housework to do, and the Revolution brought with it infection and disease, which made childbirth newly dangerous. These factors more than justified her position as a total dependent. But when housework itself was almost eliminated by the industrial system, and medical advances made childbirth safer than it had ever been before, the fundamental weakness of woman's position showed up.

The period between the setting up of the factory system, and the elimination of housework as a major chore, precipitated the historical crisis that woman was plunged into. It was a tribute to women's vitality that they saw what was happening, and responded in terms of the first feminist revolution. It is a sign of the decline in vigor of the following generations that the solution was abandoned after it had been grasped. In America, the factory system became dominant during the post-Civil War period. This era marked the onset of the crisis, and roughly coincided with the emergence of feminism. During the late forties, after the feminist revolution was an accomplished fact, housework came to an end as a significant field of work. This was the time when a new generation of women retreated from the rigors of the solution that had been handed to them by an earlier, more vigorous, generation.

As the center of life left the home, the woman gradually atrophied. Very slowly, bit by bit, she became aware that she had slipped down the scale to being a dependent, as the outer world became more threatening and she began to feel helpless to do anything about it. The insecurity and helplessness led her to exploit her position as a dependent. She became a harridan, constantly reminding the male that it was his duty to support his family. There was an obvious logic to her claim, as far as the average man could see. Not being a trained social observer, and not knowing that there had been times when things were much easier for males, all he could see was that he had to bring home the bacon or she and the kids wouldn't eat. Gradually the rich interplay that had been the home life of a decently disposed man and woman, was ground down by the abrasive friction of institutionalized parasitism. More and more, the marriage vows came to appear as a business deal where a woman gave sexual and maid service in exchange for board and room.

In the course of a few generations women became total dependents, and men became total underwriters. Woman looked out at man's life in the external world and envied the greater freedom and apparent excitement. She had forgotten about the dullness and the repetitiousness of work, and wanted to share in the apparent glamour of man's life. She had lost the capacity to sense the responsibilities and the worries, nor could she remember that once she had shared them.

The fact that men had dominated her life in the past as well as the present, tended to hide the fact that, though she had always been a subordinate, she had not always been a dependent. As she became used to being a subordinate-dependent, he, of course, got used to being a master-drudge. Neither knew that they had lived through a great historical transformation which had impoverished their emotional lives while it enriched their material one. Each thought that things for man and woman were as they had always been, that this was "civilization." Yet in the so-called primitive cultures, no male had ever carried such a tremendous burden.

The historical process by which the nonwork Option for women opened up was a general one. It affected all women everywhere in advanced technological societies. But in Europe, the transformation was muted by an existing social structure, by feedback from the past. In the United States, with no traditions to inhibit it, the process we are concerned with showed itself sharply and vividly.

Initially, the scarcity of labor in colonial and frontier America tended to produce an independent woman. This woman was so heavily employed that she shared the dream of overworked men of a euphoric state of leisure. This dream was given support by the absence of an established class in which both sexes were leisured.

Given the fact that the lower classes look up for their social models, and given the fact that the United States was settled by restless misfits, malcontents, and the ambitious and aggressive in

general—people more than willing to shed a lower-class European
identity—it was inevitable that the idle woman should become an
ideal for the overworked female.

In Europe, both sexes of the upper class were idle and leisured.
In the colonies, only the upper class woman was idle. Her husband was a dynamo. His wife was put on display, as a symbol
of conspicuous consumption. The model for Americans was a
man who worked like hell and a woman who did nothing. The
overworked lower class woman accepted this symbol at face value,
and the overworked lower class man accepted the idle woman as
a symbol of success.

Given the nature of the human brain, the relentless way it
pours out symbols of one kind or another even in sleep, most of
us do not live in reality. The American settler was more prone
to fantasy than most. In the United States, everyone lived in the
fantasy of the future. Being conscious of this, we rationalized it
as a constant awareness of the ideal of "making it." In fact, we
were living in a future-directed fantasy. The abrupt appearance
on the scene of a generation that repudiates future-directedness,
a *now* generation, suddenly makes a contrast possible. We can
now see what a powerful, mesmerizing pull the elements of the
future-directed fantasy had upon us as a nation. As an element
in this fantasy, the idle woman was implanted as a social ideal
almost from infancy. It was impossible, given the model, that any
other type of ideal woman could have taken hold in the United
States.

But this idle woman, this total dependent upon the male, was
dependent in the most extraordinary way. She was the most independent dependent that had ever crossed the stage of history,
because before the technological system made her a dependent,
it had made her as independent as she had ever been. The historical process first maximized her independence, and then without transition, thrust this maximally independent woman into
total dependence. This is what produced the demanding, exploitative character of the American female. Just before she
became a dependent, she had been used to having a lot. When
she became a dependent she continued wanting and expecting a
lot.

At every stage in the colonial history of this country, labor was
scarce and, life being nasty, brutish, and short, women were in
short supply. Thus they had a double value—as women, and as
proprietors of a scarce labor value. The price of women shot up.

During the first hundred years following the Plymouth land-ing, settlers on the east coast died off like flies. The country was not an attractive place for women, and men came here alone, either as bachelors or as married men intending to get established before sending for their wives.

Women were at a premium and able to make good marriages, materially speaking. "Trading up" became standard operating procedure. Every woman could do better than she could have done in Europe. Even the indentured female could marry up into the middle class. This factor alone could account for the greater boldness of the American woman. But there were others.

The settlement of the Middle West, and then the West, was accomplished mostly by native Americans with some capital, not by newly arrived immigrants. The same forces were set in motion again. Women were dear, doubly so. But these were men of some substance. It took money to buy, load, and haul, a Conestoga wagon across the country, or purchase a ticket around the Horn. Men like this bid up the price of scarce women even higher. And while these men were pushing westward, wave after wave of new immigrants were coming into the East, all of them without women. It was not until the post World War I period shut off immigration that the pendulum swung the other way, and the natural surplus of women began to show itself. But by that time the pattern had been established.

By the time of the Civil War, the American character had long been fixed. The woman was independent and accustomed to making the best deal she could for herself. But by the end of the Civil War, in the East, the industrial system had firmly established itself and pulled the rug out from under female independence. It was industry that set the tone of life, not the upstate farmer. Men were out of the house for good, leaving the independent woman behind. The factors making for female dependence had begun to assert themselves.

But women still had a dangerous childbirth and plenty of housework to justify their existence. Indoor toilets, electric lights, central heating, automatic washers, frozen foods, and air conditioning did not become prevalent until the late forties. Though the process of creating dependent women had started in earnest in the 1860's, it was not until the 1950's that it began to dawn that the home no longer legitimized a woman's existence. She was a total dependent who did not earn her way, no matter what dollar value was put upon her homemaking services. She had quietly become the leisured lady of the American fantasy.

But though this leisured lady no longer had the opportunity to model of an idle woman as an "arrived" woman. Then technology made her dependent. Put together an independent orientation, a model of idleness, and an enforced and sudden dependency, and you have the American woman whom the European dislikes. She is a woman who expects much, expects it all from a male, and does not bother to ask whether she is worth what she wants, or gives in proportion to what she gets.

The first thing the average married woman does when she starts working in later life, is to open her own checking account. The money she makes over and above expenses goes into buying luxuries for herself. She does not contribute to the basic expenses of the house, thus freeing money for luxuries for her husband, unless she is helping to put a child through college. When she has no children to educate, she never spends her earnings on food and mortgage, which continue to be paid out of her and her husband's joint checking account. These expenses are his responsibility.

There can be little doubt that the modern American woman ventures into the world of work with distaste, even though she is anxious to relieve the boredom of housework. She is there under the compulsion of inadequate income, not out of a desire to carry a share of responsibility. The recent small increase in the female work force stems, not from the young unmarried girl, who is most vocal in the feminist movement, but from the over-forty woman who couldn't care less about equality. Those demanding the most are doing the least to alter their condition by direct action. Those who are demanding nothing are taking the most direct route to raising themselves out of personal helplessness. The statistics are very clear on that point. The young woman is avoiding work as much as possible. The older woman is seeking it. But it is the young woman who regards herself as underprivileged.

When this young girl does hit the job market it is to find a husband, not to embrace the opportunity for growth. She remains there no longer than necessary. Once she meets her man she usually stays at work long enough to amass the down payment on a house or to furnish an apartment. But if that moment does not arrive quickly enough she often finds herself "accidentally" pregnant—pill or no pill. When life conspires to see that she stays at work, she does so as a martyr.

Advertisers have learned the hard way that they must provide the modern housewife with rationalizations for her latent guilt feelings about not working. This is what accounts for the varieties there no longer than necessary. Once she meets her man she usually stays at work long enough to amass the down payment on a house or to furnish an apartment. But if that moment does not arrive quickly enough she often finds herself "accidentally" pregnant—pill or no pill. When life conspires to see that she stays at work, she does so as a martyr.

Advertisers have learned the hard way that they must provide the modern housewife with rationalizations for her latent guilt feelings about not working. This is what accounts for the varieties of soap that are deemed necessary to get the wash done. Not anyone can do the laundry, only a "home engineer." Betty Friedan relates a story of the fifties that still holds true, of an ad that told women they could bake a cake the easiest, "laziest," way ever. It went over like a ship's anchor. It made women conscious of goofing off and aroused their guilt feelings. The modern housewife knows subliminally that she is shirking a confrontation with life, but buries that knowledge in busyness. One of the reasons she stretches out housework so far—beyond the fact that she hasn't matured to the point of being able to organize work efficiently—is that she has to make it appear as a full-time job both to herself and others.

The fully employed mature woman spends 35 hours per week gainfully employed, and another 48 hours per week doing housework—a total of 83 hours per week. The young, full-time housewife, on the other hand, manages to spend 77 hours per week on housework alone—only six hours less than the working woman! In a study published in the February, 1970, issue of the *Journal of Home Economics,* authors Florence Hall and Marguerite Schroeder declare that women today spend as much time on housework as did the housewives of half a century ago who had no laborsaving machinery.

To the assertion that the female in the modern world is not pulling her own weight, the new feminists respond with a barrage of statistics. They would have us believe that there is a dramatic increase in the number and proportion of women working. There is indeed such an increase, but it is hardly dramatic. It is on the order of from "very few" to "few," not from "very few" to "many."

The chief source of this tendentiousness is the Woman's Bureau of the U. S. Department of Labor. Bending over backwards to be fair, the male chauvinists of the Department have put the Woman's Bureau in the women's hands. The result has merely been the substitution of one kind of bias for another. The whole thrust of the Woman's Bureau is to show how much of an increase in women at work there is and has been. Unfortunately they do this by showing how many women are now at work compared to how many were at work yesterday, instead of how many are at work and how many are idle at any given time. Thus, it is extremely difficult to get a figure for any given week, month, or year, that shows how many women are working as compared to how many are not, over against how many men are working and how many are not. In the brief table where this is assayed, the truth is obscured by failure to distinguish between those who are home because they have to care for young children and those who are simply there because they want to be there.

In 1968, for example, in a population of seventy million women theoretically capable of work, twenty-nine million were in the labor force on either a full- or part-time basis, and forty-one million were not. Of this forty-one million we are told that thirty-five million were keeping house while three million were in school. But of the significant thirty-five million housekeeping women, we are not told how many are at home because they are taking care of the young and how many are there for no particular reason. This is precisely the type of statistic that hides the truth where illumination is needed.

But if we look at the long-term population figures we can see through this fancy feminist camouflage. Between 1900 and 1968 the female population tripled, but the number of working women had only doubled. In 1920, 23% of adult women worked at any time, comprising at best 20% of the total work force. By 1960 with a tripled population, this 20% figure had increased to only 37% of the women working, comprising only 35% of the total work force.

Even this figure is a gross overstatement, because not all of these 35-37% worked full-time, all year round. Some of them worked full-time during only a part of the year, and others worked even at part-time jobs for only part of the year, rather than all year round.

Only 25% worked at a full-time job all year round. The others worked part-time, and part-time at part-time work. Such a work record is not very dramatic, though technically it does show growth.

In quantitative terms, of the forty-one million women out of the possible seventy million available in 1965, only twenty-six million worked at any time and forty-four million did not. Of this forty-four million with three and a half million in school, we know from other sources that roughly fourteen million were mothering children under six. That left twenty-four million with children either in school or with no children at all, who were available for employment but were not employed. What were they doing, these twenty-four million women, besides growing larger every year? An inkling of the answer is supplied by the number of women watching daytime TV during the month of February 1969. That figure was *twenty-eight million.*

In a given work week in April 1965, as far as I can calculate from a combination of several sources, 13% of all females were in school, sick, or aged; 37% were working full- or part-time; and 50% were keeping house full-time.

As against this figure, in a working population four to five million smaller (in 1968 there were only sixty-five million men available for work compared to seventy million women) 22% of the males were either in school, or sick or aged, and 78% were working—all but a fraction at full-time jobs. In addition, four million of this 78% were holding down a second job, in addition to their primary job!

Let us use another statistic, less amenable to finagling than the labor statistics, to nail down an obvious point. Though many feminists have never heard of it—so well has the male population performed its task of protecting women from reality—there is such a thing as a *dependency ratio.* This is a term used by economists to define the relationship between the number of people available for work compared to the number too young or too old to work. One way or another, either through direct support or indirect taxation, the working population picks up the check for the nonworking population; and since two-thirds of the working population consists of men, the dependency ratio is an item peculiarly significant to men.

The bad news released by the Senate Special Committee on Aging of the 91st Congress is that there has been a sharp rise in the dependency ratio, and that the trend is still going up. As recently as 1950 there were two individuals between the productive ages of 18 and 64 to support every child under 18. The ratio is now three to two instead of two to one.

Moreover, as we are here only considering the dependency of youth, without regard to the dependency of age, and the age of 18 is no longer a realistic division between productive and non-productive age, we are drastically understating the case. Just as men past 18 are to be found in college and in the army, making the average age of work much higher, so is 65 as a retirement age unrealistic. In recent years, almost half the men beginning to receive Social Security retirement benefits, were under 65.

Combining these two factors—the trend for young men to

remain dependent long past 18, and the trend for older men to become dependent before age 65—we are rapidly heading towards a one to one dependency ratio, with one worker supporting one dependent. If this one worker is predominantly male, as he now is, this new leisure will become an added weight to the cross that working men already bear, while it will be a boon to everyone else—until the year 2010, when the excess of dependents over workers will make the system break down. So the increase in percentage of working women which the neo-feminists would have us celebrate—a mere 5% in 1968 as against 1967—is hardly enough to cause unbridled joy. Especially since this slight change for the better was not a change in the direction of greater social stability.

The increase which the feminists tout with such heraldry happens to be among older, married women, not among the young women where it is needed, even though it is the young female who makes up the cadres of feminist activists. If female parasitism is to be eliminated and an historical crisis averted, it is the young female who must change, and change drastically. So far they are conspicuously shirking the work of baking the pie, while they are stridently demanding a greater slice of it.

Prior to World War I the stereotypical woman worker was young and unmarried. Today, she is middle-aged and married. In 1900 the median age of a woman worker was 26; by 1968 it was 40.

Among the 45 to 64 age group the labor force participation was more than twice as great in 1968 as it was in 1940. During the same period the proportion of those under 25 in the work force dropped from 31 to 23%.

Part of this drop is attributable to extended schooling, but most of it can be attributed to a cop-out through early marriage. Today, more girls marry at age 18 than at any other age, and half have snagged a source of support by age 20. Thus, for many, there is a direct progression from dependency on the father to dependency on the husband, without even a nodding acquaintance with the world of work.

I have no statistics or studies to buttress this observation, but it seems to me and to others that of all those women who are working, generally it is only the older ones who are really "working." The younger ones are merely "gainfully employed," many of them owing their jobs to the fact that their employers are desperate for help and couldn't get better qualified assistants. It is not too extravagant to say that the majority of young female workers are taking their checks under false pretenses, doing as little as they can for it. Companies staffed mostly by married men experience an unusually high turnover of girls.

Moreover, while the young woman is marking time with the benefit of a paycheck, her work is often unbelievably irresponsible. She really doesn't believe she ought to be at work at all, and so she doesn't care how well she performs. She does not want to work. She feels she has a right not to work, that it is some man's duty to support her. Even if she is unmarried, her attitude towards work is that of "Daddy's little helper," not of a mature woman responsible for herself. The responsibility is the man's; she is just helping out temporarily.

All of this irresponsibility she rationalizes by the fantasy that men do not like capable, intelligent women. This may have been true once, but it is not widely true now. Women have been aware that there was a time when men disliked educated women; but they failed to note that educated women were not the exclusive objects of men's hostility. Such hostility was also directed at the minority of educated men, by the majority of uneducated men. It was not a specifically anti-educated woman hostility, but an anti-intellectual hostility, one which women mistakenly took to be anti-feminine.

In today's world, it is only the man who is denied education, or cannot absorb it, who still resents brainy women. The brainy man wants a brainy woman. As one ascends the status ladder, one narrows down one's peer group. It is a risk of social advancement. The woman who is loath to give up some males as potential husband material must pay the price of reduced chance of social advancement. But it is time for women to realize that not all males are potential husband material. The lowbrow male is not a suitable candidate for the highbrow female. This recognition has long been overdue.

Rationalizations such as this have hidden the dysfunction that occurs when women deny all responsibility but the responsibility of maternity. Life has polarized unhealthily for both sexes, creating extreme disequilibrium in the emotional economy. Women have come to live on an island of maternity and regard it as normal; men have come to live on an island of work and regard that as normal. Both are impoverished. And man's bondage has been doubled by the peculiarities of modern industry. His so-called duty to his family requires him to carry total responsibility for them. In order to do that, he must submit slavishly to the excessive demands of the work system. Having submitted, he is then an object of contempt to those for whom the sacrifice was made. Mother finds him lacking in the qualities of a film idol. Junior finds him a hypocrite and a money grubber.

The neo-feminists' demands of equality—by which they mean all of man's rights but none of his responsibilities—have exacerbated a bad situation. And when the foreign observer sees the American male as a weak man, dominated by his women, he is making a slight error in judgement. The American is no weaker than the European man; he has simply been brainwashed into accepting a sense of values which is serving the selfish, but unhealthy, purposes of the female, to his own detriment. The American male is a drudge, not because he lacks the guts to stand up to his wife, but because he thinks it is right not to. He really believes that his first duty in life is to support women, rather than to take care of himself!

He is oblivious to the fact that this belief is instilled in each new generation of males by the party most prejudiced, and least able to write wise legislation—women. Mother and teacher are bringing up junior to "be nice"—that is, subservient to women's purposes. He, the father, unwittingly compounds the error by spoiling his daughter, by bringing her up to expect to be served by other men as he serves her.

Thus we have arrived at the absolutely baffling situation in which the female—atrophied and impoverished by the movement of history, less mature, shallower, more fantasy-ridden and selfish than she ever was before—writes the legislation being accepted by men! Her values are the dominant values of society, though she herself is a subordinate.

There is objective proof that men and women live in a host-parasite relationship, beyond my subjective perception of it. A 1965 survey of women in Chicago revealed that the women perceived men as standing outside the basic family unit. According to the woman's lights, the basic unit was *herself, her* children, and *her* home. Men were seen as outside this unit, as providers or suppliers of income.

The survey asked the question: "What are the most important roles of a woman?" The answer was: (1) mother; (2) homemaker; (3) *wife*. The man was seen as: (1) *breadwinner;* (2) father; (3) husband.

Her first duty was to her offspring, her second duty was to her nest, her last duty was to her husband. He lost out, not only to the children, but to the sticks and stones that comprised the nest.

His first duty was to make money, his second duty was to father the child, and his last duty (or privilege?) was to enjoy her favors.

Everybody knew that women expected to be supported and that men expected to support. But only when this knowledge was seen in its rank order to other things did its true significance become manifest. The relationship between men and women—which one had always assumed to be more important than all others—had so badly deteriorated that, impoverished and parasitical as it had come to be, woman saw it as normal! Was it the shock of recognizing a horrible truth that compelled everyone to laugh this study off, as just another joke in the battle of the sexes? Apparently all remembrance of a healthier relationship had passed completely out of human consciousness. But if the core relationship between the sexes can become distorted without anyone sensing it, and we can accept this distortion as normal, how much of a grasp do we have on anything else?

There was new proof at hand that our old ways were no longer good enough. Equality had been pushed to its logical conclusion in Sweden and had not solved the historical crisis. In Sweden, sexual freedom as well as political and economic equality is already the reality that American feminists yearn for. Sexual relations before marriage are the norm, babies born out of wedlock are routinely announced in the newspaper, contraceptive techniques are taught in the schools, and diaphragms, loops, and pills are available to young girls without restrictions as to age. In Sweden all the equality a system could deliver has been delivered, yet women are still not equal.

According to one leading Swedish feminist, Inger Becker, Swedish women have not accepted more responsibility than do women in more traditional setups. The parasitical side of Swedish women is now emerging clearly. Girls still elect easier courses in school, and young women prepare for no skills but take on any unskilled work in the expectation of being supported by a man. According to Miss Becker, they are still practising entrapment, pulling men into marriage by "accidental" pregnancies. One third of the births occur before the marriage is eight months old. Swedish women are still using their bodies as their primary means of support. The reason? "The predatory relationship continues," she says, "because women are just lazy. It is still much easier to marry a doctor than to become one."

Having had a chance to study equality at work, another Swedish feminist, Eva Mossberg, also saw the flaw. "[Women] can't expect equality while they are expecting the male to cherish and protect them," she exclaimed. "If you [women] want equality, you can't ask for favors because of your sex."

The Russian experience lent further proof to the proposition that the slogan of equality had played itself out. In Marxist equalitarian thinking, prostitution was supposed to be a result of the exploitation of the poor brought about by capitalism. Yet in contemporary Russia, where no one starves for lack of a job, there are still women who obviously prefer prostitution to gainful employment, much to the distress of the establishment ideologists. If prostitution is a vice, it is not one fundamentally imposed by grim necessity.

There can be little doubt that in the past, when society forced on the female the need to work as well as to wive, it unwittingly gave her a perfect insurance policy for survival, in the same way it did for the male. But when modern conditions made it possible for women to avoid work, it gave them the means to cripple themselves. The Option is a hot potato. By means of it, the modern woman can kill herself without ever realizing that she has signed her own death warrant. What else could account for the gaping difference between the maturity levels of men and women that we see today? We must acknowledge that the Option has not been a social success. Women do not have enough innate aggression to use it wisely. To restore them as well as society to health, the Option to work or wive must be eliminated. It must be made mandatory for all women to work and accept responsibility. This requirement will force woman back into a healthy contact with reality, a contact she shrinks from because of her natural timidity.

Admittedly, value judgements have played an important part in this analysis. Unlike Part I, where hard fact allowed objectivity, we are here dealing with insights and intuition, and with relative values. But there is one hard fact in support of the foregoing, to which we shall now turn.

What Every Man Knows

If there is one thing the biological approach to human behavior clearly demonstrates, it is the intricacy of the mesh between males and females. If the male and female are not designed to function in a complementary way, then we know nothing about biology.

The degree and complexity of the interlock is something to marvel at. There has been a deliberate design here, which has been undergoing constant refinement over the millenia. The two sexes are meant to function as one whole. Each is dependent upon the other in critical ways. There is more than romantic and poetic meaning to this thought. From the basic, locking, design of the sexual parts, up through the morphology of the body, to the morphology of the mind, and beyond the body to the different but complementing roles they play in society, each sex is incomplete without the other. Only a couple is immortal; the single sex perishes.

Therefore, if one finds an area in which the sexes do not mesh, where they are not functionally complementary, one is entitled to the legitimate suspicion that something isn't working right. If complementarity and harmony are the evolutionary goals, as they obviously are, the lack of complementarity and harmony must be regarded as abnormal and dysfunctional. And if one finds a failure to mesh in a crucially important area, one must consider the dysfunction a serious one.

There is one such area in contemporary life in which the sexes are not in harmony, and that is in their sexuality. The sexes are not meshing well sexually. This failure is bad in itself as well as bad for what it implies for the whole relation between the two sexes which is built on it. I believe that this lack of mesh in sexual relationships is a socially caused abnormality which is by that very reason controllable, even though marriage counselors have always accepted it as part of the given facts. Millions of years of evolution have made the sexes mesh like fine gears at the biological level; it seems unthinkable, therefore, that this abnormality should be biological and unalterable. But if it is not innate it must be social, and within our power to change. In this it is like feminine immaturity, which we have always taken as biologically immutable, rather than as a sign of a socially caused neurosis which it was in our power to correct.

The dysfunction which strikes me as a major proof of the seriously maladjusted relationship between the sexes shows up in the curve of sexual drive of adults. Biology calls for them to be in harmony, but in fact they are not. The adult male has a downward curve while the adult female curve is rising. In other words, while the male is experiencing decreased sexual desire with advancing age, the female is experiencing increased desire as she gets older. The male peaks at about age 18, the female at about age 35. Something is wrong here.

This is not to say that males on a downward curve cannot successfully copulate with females on an upward one; obviously, they can. But the differences either deny the principle of biological harmony or point to a maladjustment in social roles. I take the latter to be the case. I believe that excessive responsibility is suppressing male desire, and that insufficient responsibility leading to an unhealthy fantasy life is overstimulating female sexual desire. Life has pushed male and female out of step with each other. Let us review what we know and try to find out where things are going wrong, in order to pinpoint corrective action.

We know that up to adolescence, the central nervous system of the human female develops faster than the male's. We interpret this to mean that nature has programmed the female to perform her most important task, reproduction, as early as possible, before she has a chance to get killed off. As the time draws near for her to perform this task, the male suddenly experiences a spurt in the growth of his nervous system so that he too is ready to play his part. His spurt shows up as an increase in mental agility, a desire to set up on his own, and a drive to copulate. The female has been made ready and receptive. He is driven by increased aggression to take the initiative. His drive is greater than hers at this point, but that is all right. Although she is experiencing no increased tension, she, too, is ready.

At this point, we can accept a difference in sexual drive as normal. But from here on, why should her drive increase while his declines? Why do they not both decline, having presumably accomplished their reproductive tasks?

It is in the cards that his should decline somewhat. Having impregnated a female he now turns his attention to safeguarding her during her period of defenselessness. But since she has already been fertilized, why should she experience more rather than less desire now? As can be seen in the housecat, her mothering instincts decline after the first litter. Having completed her task she no longer has need for a strong maternal drive. Nonetheless, she grows more sexy while he grows less so. What has happened?

I think two things have happened simultaneously: The male sex drive is depressed even more than we should expect by the demands of fatherhood, while the release from responsibility stimulates the female's sexual appetite sufficiently to reverse the natural biological decline. In this overstimulation of the female and oversuppression of the male I see, in capsule form, the present social disequilibrium of the emotional economy. What biology harmonized, society has antagonized.

There are both long-term and short-term causes for this situation. In the short run we are experiencing the overzealousness of females determined to redress the balance of many generations of sexual denial. The pendulum of history has swung to the other extreme. For the first time in history, the female has been freed from the fear of untimely pregnancy by the pill. Simultaneously with her new freedom, she has become aware that the aberrations of Puritanism were responsible for cheating her out of sexual pleasure. In addition to these two factors, the feminists have made women suspicious in general concerning the sufficiency of their share of the spoils; as a result, we have the spectre of the female sex gourmand—a creature determined to "get hers" come what may. Until the pendulum settles down again, female excess will be the norm.

There is another reason for this female excess: Getting a husband is the most critical challenge in her life, even in our modern world, because a husband is the ticket to the cop-out. You can't goof off without a man to foot the bills. Success requires self-discipline. This is one time in a woman's life when she actively enforces such self-discipline. If this period is unduly prolonged, if she experiences difficulty in getting a husband, she may build up quite a head of resentment against males for having forced her to undergo such a trial. Once she has run the gauntlet and survived, she is likely to spend the rest of her life exacting revenge from the unwitting unfortunate she has married. Two of the ways in which she will do this are to find him sexually inadequate, and lacking in earning power.

But most women are not motivated by a desire for vengeance. Once she has passed her test, the average woman simply relaxes and forgets about it. Now, freed from all future worries about the feeding and shelter of herself and her infants, she is in a position to become playful—and that is precisely the way she gets. Though she appears to have more cares than ever, she moves toward irresponsibility. Not having to submit to the chastening embrace of reality, she can and does live in fantasy. In that fantasy world—exacerbated by the mass media—she dwells on the pleasures of sex, and comes to expect a level of performance that a reality-dwelling man cannot deliver. Thus, the female soars along on a constantly rising sex curve.

But the error is not all on her side. The male curve is also skewed down further than it ought to be. Upon marriage, the male experiences a dramatic increase in sexual inhibition, which comes as much as a surprise to him as it does to his spouse. As a bachelor, he had thought that in marriage he would have it made. Instead, her new spontaneity is matched by his loss of it. Her new freedom has become his surprising loss of freedom. Her irresponsibility has become his responsibility. The key word is *responsibility*. The key concept is its movement to a new location. In the modern world, marriage liberates the female and enslaves the male, in a way and to a degree unprecedented in history.

In Paleolithic days, marriage made no changes in the life of the hunter, except to enrich it. He went about his business just as though he were a bachelor. Hunting was still as much a sport as a chore. The share of meat the female got would have gone into the community pot anyway, primitives being natural communists.

The same cannot be said of hunting's modern equivalent—work, and its corollary, responsibility. Modern man's work load and responsibility load are the most effective sexual depressants ever invented. Few marriage counselors have ever understood the full significance of the effect work, responsibility, and worry have on the sexual drive, although every married male is privately aware of it. It is one of those common experiences which have been taken for granted tacitly for so long that their full significance is not grasped.

Not that any kind of work or responsibility necessarily acts as a sexual depressant. Indeed, some kinds of work under certain kinds of conditions are powerful sexual stimulants. What I am asserting is that work and responsibility in our modern technological society are sexual depressants for two reasons. The first one, that males accept self-serving feminine values as their own, I have already discussed. The second, that man is oppressed by a massive bureaucracy from which there is no escape, is important enough to warrant separate analysis, which follows in the next chapter.

At this point I should like to discuss in a general way how it is possible for work and responsibility to act as sexual depressants.

Any number of things can turn off the sex switch. Humans may be sexually active to a far greater extent than other creatures, but they still experience even more powerful drives, and when these collide with sex, sex loses out. Hunger, thirst, fatigue, danger, fear, worry, absorption in thought or study, are some of the stimuli that turn off the sexual apparatus. In general, any stimulus of a crisis nature will eliminate all competing stimuli, in order that all bodily energy can be focused on the challenge. Man's adrenaline pattern clearly shows that meeting crisis is his biological specialty, to the extent that a generalist has a specialty. Our crisis-meeting mechanisms are also our hangup.

Hunting was our earliest racial experience of crisis, and our crisis-meeting mechanisms evolved out of this collective experience. Work also evolved out of hunting. But the hunting crisis and the work crisis are two different things. The insecurity and uncertainty of the modern work experience, and distorting pressures exerted by the competitive rat race, act as extended crises which turn man off sex, despite medical plans, accident plans, retirement plans, and all other cradle-to-grave security plans. For the same reasons he is also turned off culturally, artistically, emotionally, and philosophically. The hunting crisis was of short duration and this is the type of crisis we are programmed for. The work crisis is permanent, and we have not been programmed for it. Having to face it nonetheless, our response is trancelike: We rivet our attention on the crisis and stay riveted for the duration with all other stimuli shut out. Man, at this point in history, lives his entire adult life in a condition of permanent crisis, and is more or less permanently turned off, sexually speaking. Not

only do his worries and responsibilities leave little room for the
lighter side of his nature, but every orgasm is accompanied by
the penis-shrinking knowledge that he may just have forged another $1,500-per-year link in his chain. It costs, as of the latest
1970 estimates, $30,000 to rear one child to age 18—without the
frills, just for meat and potatoes and protection from the rain.
If one throws in the frills that are commonplace among middle-
brow families, and throws in the cost of college at the rate of
$5,000 per year, we can see that we are seriously underestimating
the bite. Few lectures on sin or venereal disease can match this
for effectiveness, in inhibiting the male sex urge! Little wonder
that 75% of the 100,000 people per year now seeking sterilization
are men.

It does nothing to assuage man's growing sense of entrapment
to understand that while he is being alienated from his deepest
self, his wife is discovering the full depth of her soul; or that,
while he is becoming imprisoned, she is gaining freedom. A
woman has some twenty-five to thirty opportunities in her life to
prove her femininity by bearing children. Some women have to
be restrained from using them all. But there are few men so
economically successful that they can bear with equanimity more
than two $1,500-per-annum permanent increases in overhead. In
plain fact, most men worry about their ability to support children.
Women are not so burdened. They leave that worry to him, and
see no connection between it and his sexual coolness.

Nor do they see any connection between "their thing" and the
soaring property tax. The first two children fit into the existing
school facilities—if one is living in an established community and
not in a new town. The third child requires the building of a
new school. In 1969, my community, Upper Saddle River, New
Jersey, spent 72% of its tax collections on schools, and only 28%
on all other costs combined. This means that $720 out of every
$1,000 tax bill went for feminine fulfillment, and will continue
to do so for the next thirty years until the school bonds are paid
off. (This item is in addition to the basic $1,500 per year.) If the
wives of the village had been more interested in the outside
world, and less in copping out, the tax bill might have been $280.

It is true that once the fertility goddess finally got the word that
there was a direct connection between her self-expression and the
local tax rate, she became content with fewer rites. This apparently happened in 1957, the year of the high point in the zoom-
ing birth rate, with 25.3 births per thousand. In 1958 it began
to drop and has dropped constantly until 1968, when the birth

rate was 17.4 per thousand—which is about the low of the depression years. It will undoubtedly drop even further, but even that low represented 3,470,000 new people. The damage had already been done.

In the same month in which the above statistic was published, the area newspaper also carried an article on living costs in the New York City-Northern New Jersey area. "If you are a factory worker in the New York-North New Jersey area trying to keep up with the proverbial Joneses, forget it," the article said. "The Joneses can't keep up with themselves." The rest of the article informed the reader that it cost a family of four people $10,513 to live moderately in the area. "Moderately" meant like a suburban factory worker. The actual factory standard take-home pay for the area was $6,258. The difference between what this family had to spend and what it needed to keep up with the blue-collar Joneses, could have been bridged by a full-time working wife, but only a few of these families had one. The difference between what was available and what was needed was, of course, carried in tension by the husband—who was also, incidentally, experiencing another one of his spells of impotence. His wife's negative opinion of him was shared by her children, who couldn't understand why they couldn't go to day camp along with the other kids. They came to the conclusion that their father was cheap.

Failure to be a hero to his children and a Don Juan to his wife will not be the only shortcomings to accrue to our man's account. He will already have noticed, if he was at all perceptive, that there was a radical contradiction in the modes by which masculinity was projected in TV stories and commercials. In the fictional part of the program he will have been depicted as a rough, tough, private eye or spy. In the commercial, he will be pictured as a bungling incompetent, or, for variety, as a chump. The typical American male, as viewed through the eyes of the typical American advertising copywriter, is a fool. If this characterization were occasional, it could be written off as a chance occurrence. Everyone realizes that a fool makes easy copy. But the monotonous repetition of the man-as-fool theme indicates that the ad men are getting a positive reaction to it. The audience recognizes the figure and responds to it. This recognition is not based upon perversity, but is a kind of subliminal recognition of man's true position. Man is, in the contemporary world, a servant-for-hire. Servants are submissive. But a man who fantasizes himself as a rugged individualist and in reality functions as a servant, really is a fool.

This is especially true when he spends his life bound to a job the benefits of which go primarily to wife and child—neither of whom is particularly appreciative, or even aware of what their maintenance really costs him. The sole satisfaction he gets out of his work is the knowledge that he doesn't quit under fire, that whatever the system dishes out, he can take it. It is no secret that present-day working conditions permit little fulfillment, except for a lucky few. The great number of books on the subject of alienation attests to this. Most jobs permit neither work satisfaction, nor masculine validation. Not only has most hard labor disappeared with the advent of the machine; what little hard labor is left, he no longer likes to do. Contemporary man is a white-collar man who buys the services of those who cannot, like he, avoid hard labor. Just as his wife has forgotten the time when she was not a dependent, he has forgotten that there once was a time when men took pleasure in flexing their muscles. Modern man does not mourn the loss of hard labor, though he does mourn the loss of the psychic satisfaction that went with it.

Democratic equality for wives—and permissiveness for children —has resulted in a precipitous decline of male authority within the home as well as at the job. Yet the woman's need to look up to her husband, and the boy's need to respect his father, has not changed. Both needs continue to be as strong as ever, only now they remain unsatisfied.

For the first time in history, youngsters are unsure as to whether the man is, or should be, the head of the house. Vance Packard reports a newspaper article in which the young people surveyed gave a majority vote for the proposition that the man was *not* the head of the house. My local paper carried the same kind of survey, which arrived at the conclusion that the man *should be* the head of the house. Yet one boy declared wistfully, with a wisdom beyond his years, that women change somehow after marriage, and it didn't work. I don't think children should be deciding that issue. I think they should be presented with clear, unmistakable models, and realize unequivocally that the man is and should be head of the household.

As matters stand now, the only authority the children see being exercised, is the authority of the mother running her house. It is understandable that they are confused. But the decline of the authority of husbands and fathers is not a permanent feature of the conventional home; it is one destined to be reversed when men understand the necessity for doing so.

The man's attempts to allow other members of his family a

chance at self-expression and individual development has created a vagueness in standards where clarity is essential. Young males, especially, are confused about what is expected of them and show this in many ways. Though many of them have reacted against the torpor of male life, there is still an obvious increase in the number of passive, dependent males, and this trend is unhealthy.

The gulf that separates the boy from the adult male world can never have been so difficult to cross as it is today. The boy must view the chasm with great anxiety, for never has the development of competence been so trying. With the possible exception of warrior cultures like the Sioux, who lived on poor land, or the Eskimo, there may never have been a culture which demanded so much from its young males as does ours.

At first sight this seems rather exaggerated. One of the tests a little Sioux boy had to pass was to run five miles through the hot desert with a mouthful of water without swallowing a drop. This test separated the men from the boys so well that the Sioux were obliged to invent a male squaw role, not so much for their homosexual boys, as for their heterosexual boys who couldn't pass the warrior tests.

The young American boy may be spared the physical agonies of such puberty rites, but the psychological gauntlet he runs is just as fearsome. The Sioux boy was a Stone Age boy. When his tests were over he fit into a Stone Age culture. The modern boy comes into the world a Stone Age baby, just like the Sioux boy, but when his rites of passage are over he must fit himself into the 20th century.

In all cultures, the fear that little boys will not grow up to be men is more severe than that little girls will not grow up to be women. Among warrior cultures, as well as in modern American culture, this fear is pervasive. It is no wonder that some Sioux boys copped out and became squaws, or that more and more American boys become homosexual. The little boy sees he will have to put out to join the world of men. The little girl knows she will coast into the adult world of women without a ruffle. The boy will pass through a psychological crucible on the way to manhood, and when he reaches it, he will have to prove it over and over again. Yesterday's feats do not excuse tomorrow's failures. In the test of his manhood, he is never a winner.

Even the sexual role of the male is more challenging than the female's. He must produce an erection to copulate; she can fake her way through. Failure to produce an erection at the appointed moment is for him tantamount to failure as a man—in front of the woman. Yet a worried man cannot get an erection or arouse a female. The fear of not being able to perform on cue is one of the chief fears of the homosexual hankering after heterosexuality. Dr. Bieber of the New York Medical College concludes that homosexuals avoid intercourse with women because "they have developed overwhelming fears of their sexual capacity," which means, of getting an erection at the right time. Psychiatrist Harry Hershman says, "A woman poses a tremendous problem to him, for only she can expose him as defective in the role of a man."

The homosexual is not the only one disconcerted by the female. According to both Packard and Brenton, the heterosexual male is too. Her aggressiveness in matters sexual, instead of delighting the male whose sex fantasies have now come down to earth, alarm him. Modern women are becoming "critical consumers of male performance." Theodore Reik declared himself amazed at the way "women, more and more, are taking over the active role in sex." Man's sexual performance is increasingly being judged in terms of his ability to give sexual pleasure, not to impregnate. Considering that recent research has shown that woman is capable of practically unlimited orgasms, and coming at a time when responsibility is depressing his sexual capacity, this is a situation wide open to abuse. It may be appropriate to judge prostitutes on their ability to deliver sexual pleasure, but not anyone else. The male does not need this cross to bear in addition to the ones already laid on his back. Especially is this true when the same research that demonstrated woman's unlimited orgasmic capacity also showed that her best source of sexual pleasure is self-masturbation, followed, secondly, by a male masturbating her. Third and last as her source of pleasure is the male penis. Under these circumstances, one must question a woman's fitness to be a judge of sexual capacity, her own or anyone else's. This unlimited quality to current feminine sexuality is explained by the fact that her fantasies are unencumbered by the tempering quality of an encounter with reality. She lives in a pornographic state of mind.

At the opening of the century, when the feminists were hitting their stride for the first time, sympathetic male writers gave their cause a boost by writing plays like *The Ten Pound Look,* and *What Every Woman Knows.* In the first of these plays the downtrodden wife of a rich industrialist discovers that she can be free by learning to operate a typewriter, which cost ten pounds. In the second, the woman learns that the authoritarian husband had dependecy needs for her. These themes did much to persuade many men that a system whereby an oppressive male could enslave a woman because the law recognized no human rights for her, was unsound and unjust and should be changed.

I should like to point out that the historical conditions that justified these themes have passed into history and structural inequality no longer exists to any serious extent. The pendulum has now swung too far in the other direction and it is the male who is oppressed, though not legally. Support for this claim is given by the absolute triviality of the targets the neo-feminists now attack. The division of the "Help Wanted" columns into "Male" and "Female" did nothing to inhibit women from applying for jobs as garbage collectors. Nor will pushing their way into "Men Only" bars give women greater access to either alcohol or men. Even as symbols of isolated pockets of structural inequality, these targets only serve to illustrate how little serious structural inequality still exists. One fully expects the activists to barge into the men's room next and demand the installation of appropriate facilities.

How can one balance sex-oriented Help Wanted ads, and Men Only bars, in the scales against alimony for perfectly healthy and childless women with an aversion to helping themselves? The appropriate theme for this age is not, "What Every Woman Knows," but "What Every Man Knows" about feminine parasitism, and how men can get out from under professional Claudias who refuse to grow up. More equality for women, in the feminist sense of equality, means greater parasitism for the female. It means throwing the scales of justice further out of balance. The ludicrousness of the contemporary demand for "more" is dramatized by the recent report of a man who sued Pan American Airlines for access to a job as a steward. He complained that the airlines were violating his civil rights by hiring only women for the job! His suit was supported by the Civil Liberties Union.

Sooner or later, whatever attitudes a man married with, there comes a time when he suspects he is being had. Sooner or later he realizes that she lacks any conception of the human cost of "things," and may even despise him for having lost his dignity in their acquisition; he feels himself maturing while his wife remains a girl. When he married her, she was a good friend as well as a lover, but that now she is a stranger and a drag. Or possibly worse; for if she is insensitive to the changes that have taken place in him, it must be that she is indifferent to them, feeling that his burdens are *his* cross to bear.

Nothing goads the feminists more than the assertion that women do no significant work. Their vexation at this charge has led women to put a legal price tag on housework. It is not my intention here to maintain that housework has no economic value. I am well aware of the time and energy a woman can spend in rearing children and housewifely duties. There is no doubt that during the time from just before childbirth to the time a child enters school, the woman is heavily and even excessively employed.

What I *am* saying, however, is that before and after this period housework cannot be regarded as a task equal to that of full-time work for pay in the outside world. It has some economic value, but not of comparable magnitude. The average home can be cleaned in three hours a day. Food preparation for breakfast and dinner need take no more than another hour and a half. That many women spend more at these tasks testifies to their lack of self-discipline and organization, not to the inherent difficulty of the task.

The principal difference between housework and outside work for pay is that housework is postponable. At this moment, a weekday morning, seventeen million women are watching TV. Before I stop work for the day, twenty-eight million will have watched. I submit that none of these women is living on a schedule that cannot be altered at will, or ignored altogether, if the woman so desires. How many men have that choice? Even given the boredom of housework, which is no more boring than many types of paid work, it is still largely free from compulsion. It does not have to be done. Paid work does. This very element of compulsion makes work a source of growth (as well as a source of alienation). There is no growth without challenge, though there can be too much challenge or the wrong kind. The difference between working in the world and working in the home, is that the former stimulates growth and the latter does not.

Compulsion is the key to why the charities women engage in cannot be taken seriously as a substitute for work. A woman can walk away from them whenever she likes, and much of this activity cannot be taken seriously in the first place. I know of a twenty-member woman's group that collected items for a charity sale, for total proceeds of twelve to fourteen dollars. Each must have spent at least one dollar in auto expenses and at least two hours in work. If they had done no work and simply chipped in the auto expenses they could have raised $20 without effort. If each had worked during a lunch period in a local restaurant for the minimum wage of $1.50 per hour, they would have raised $60. This type of activity simply cannot be taken seriously as an alternative to work.

Before delving more deeply into this strange world of work, there is one other distortion rooted in excessive dependency upon the male, which must be discussed: The dependent woman must reach out for life *through* the male.

Women may be dependent but they are not inert; they have wants, wishes, aspirations, and drives. In a position of subordinate dependency, they must channel these drives through the male. This creates an anomalous situation in which there appears to be one body playing host to two personalities, or one life inhabited by two spirits. The woman tenants a man almost like a fetus tenants her body, only there is a time limit on the fetus and none on her tenancy of the male. I am reminded of the many science-fiction films in which creatures from outer space take over human bodies to fit themselves into the scheme of things on this planet. Figuratively, in order to follow their own inner dynamics, women do the same thing—they compete for the use of a body that is already inhabited. An alternate illustration is provided by the plastic sleeves built into the walls of rooms housing dangerously radioactive material. A technician standing safely outside the walls can slip his arms into the sleeves and manipulate the deadly stuff inside the housing, without going in. I see woman manipulating man in this way, and man, because he thinks it is right, tolerates it.

Once we become conscious of the fact that a dependent woman has no choice but to manipulate the male in order to achieve her goals, we see what is wrong with this kind of relationship. In the emotional economy, it would be more efficient for women to touch life directly rather than indirectly through the male.

This type of manipulation is both conscious and unconscious. The nagging that goes with conscious manipulation is, while tiresome, open and aboveboard. The man can resist it. But the unconscious manipulation is insidious.

Men respond to their own unconscious processes simply by taking the actions and the moves these processes dictate. The energy in these processes is discharged without anyone being the wiser. But the fantasies and unshaped longings of women, especially of immature women who are still trying to find their identities, cannot be discharged by direct action. The woman must discharge them through the male. But he is only partially compliant, and her psyche is always alive with unexpressed energy constantly seeking an outlet in manipulation. The conscious woman wants her husband to be dominant; but the unconscious woman cannot allow him to be, because she must be able to manipulate him.

It is this inability to discharge her psychic energy directly that accounts for the wife who makes a career of remolding her husband. She is not even aware of doing it. But she is really trying to refashion him into a more perfect instrument of her own self-expression. It is sometimes difficult to see why a given woman accepts a given man, when she had the choice of others, and then dedicates herself to doing him over completely. If she succeeds, she often despises him for having allowed it to happen. Her conscious mind reacts adversely to what her unconscious mind has done. When she fails, she is thoroughly frustrated and expresses that frustration in objectionable personality traits.

Where the historical stage of evolution does not permit the female in dependency much chance at individuation, the situation is, paradoxically, tolerable. Worse things are happening to the people involved to notice it. But where individuation is possible, the extreme dependency of the woman is an obstacle to growth. We are in such an epoch now. The extreme dependency of the woman inhibits her own growth, as well as placing a debilitating, inhibiting burden on the male. She has infected him with her crisis. This is the answer to the question posed at the opening of this chapter, as to why the sexual interest curves of the male and female are not in harmony. The woman, not being sexually restrained by responsibility, soars in fantasy into a pornographic world. The man being overburdened by worry, has been switched off sexually. To shift some responsibility to the female, would be to put a brake on her sexual fantasies. To relieve the male of some responsibility would relax him, release some playful energy, remove a physiological restriction on his sexual interest, and move him back towards the woman in sexual interest. The implications of this line of reasoning for the sexually interested female are obvious.

The World of Work

It has been asserted that there are two sources of tension in male life: the feminine value system he has adopted as his own, and the world of work. At home he confronts the distorting effects of technology indirectly, for it is the peculiar role that technology has allotted to women that makes her what she is. At work he confronts the ogre directly.

The indirect effects of technology on man have already been sketched. We shall now attempt to delineate the direct effects. To attempt an analysis of the economic system in one chapter is, in a sense, ludicrous. This is an area which has occupied many of the best minds of every generation, with inconclusive results. But our subject, the power relationship between man and woman, allows us to limit ourselves to an analysis of the effects of the work world on that relationship. It is a crucial area for inquiry.

Given the fact that man's biological need to work has been subtly corrupted into the social dictum to support women, it follows that when man's private wishes as to the kind of work he would like to spend his life at, conflict with what is right—that is, work that will securely support women—they must be put away with his other boyhood toys. Thus, having dampened man's flow of fantasies by subjecting them to a stiff dose of reality, the female can comfortably retreat into *her* world of fantasy, secure in the knowledge that she can dream on without inhibition.

The time arrives when the properly indoctrinated male leaves the feminine environment of home and school, for what must surely be a masculine environment of work. If he enters the blue-collar world he will be lucky, for that world is by and large a masculine world. He will be expected to conform to job discipline, but because management does not expect him to like it, he will have the freedom to express his hostility to work verbally. He will also be free to express the coarse side of his nature. This important safety valve will be denied his white-collar brother, who will be expected to radiate management attitudes, even in trivial paper-shuffling assignments.

But there will be an even bigger disappointment in store for the white-collar man: he will find that the world of work he is going to spend his life in is as feminine as the world of home and school. He will find that, at first, being an employee is no different from being a son or a student. He will be graded on his performance. The world of white-collar work may be a masculine world for the upper management and the salesmen, but it is still a feminine place for everyone else. The same qualifications which made him a good son, a model student, an attractive date, and will soon make him a responsible husband, will also make him an acceptable employee.

If, by some fluke of fortune, little of the feminine sense of values has taken root in him, and he enters the world of work with obsolete masculine attitudes, he will have to shed them quickly. His immediate boss will resent them fiercely, as the young blood might be spotted by higher authority as a comer and be a candidate for the boss's slot.

This has been a standard academic criticism of the business world ever since William Whyte articulated it in 1956, in his by now classic book *The Organization Man*. It expresses not only the outsider's attitude; thinkers within the business community itself agree with it. One of the leading personnel men in the country also admits it as an outstanding problem of business, one urgently awaiting solution. Stanley Herman, in his recent book, *The People Specialists*, says that "passivity, dependence, submissiveness, seem to be the hallmarks of 'good employees.'" He also quotes another practitioner who states unequivocally that "In most corporations, maturity is not a prized quality."

There is no doubt but that world of work, like the world of school and home, wants femininity in its men. A masculine young male will undergo severe crises in his first contacts with the work world (unless he is brought in as a high-level "management trainee"). He will be fired a couple of times, or eased out in other

ways. If he is assertive enough he probably won't be hired at all—
except perhaps as a sales trainee—because the personnel man who
interviews him will resent his assertiveness and will have plenty of
theory with which to rationalize his resentments. Himself housebroken, he will resent an unbroken stallion. His overt reason will
be that a square peg in a round hole is likely to generate friction
and impede the smooth working of the system. Actually, he will
simply resent a masculine male and vent his resentment by block-
ing his entry into the company.

Threatened with life failure before he starts, the young male
will learn to lie and cheat and pretend to be something he is not.
That is the price of his survival. He will color himself bland. This
is no exaggeration as the turnover figures for young, beginning
workers show. That high turnover rate is normally interpreted as
due to the young man trying on a job like a suit of clothes. Buried
in it is the fact that many of these young men have not yet
learned to fake submissiveness, and are hoping they won't have
to, by finding a job where they can be themselves.

This crisis in getting started is complicated by the fact that the
young man is consumer-oriented, not work-oriented. He just plain
doesn't know yet how to do a job. The young of both sexes start
out by regarding a job as a place where checks are given out at
periodic intervals. It takes them awhile to adjust to the cruel im-
position of having to give something in exchange for the check.
Even the very meek ones must learn that.

But our young male will blunder through this stage, and in
doing so he will discover that his first impression was wrong.
Work is not like school. Work is hard. Though the hours are
relatively short and the work is not physically hard, it is, nonetheless, emotionally hard. It will take him two cocktails to unwind
after a day at the office, while his high school friend who became
an auto mechanic is ready to go out on the town after a hot bath
and a good meal. Paradoxically, the drain on the white-collar
man was greater than it was on the blue-collar man—and the pay
was less. In the chrome and polish of the office, the white-collar
man was living a a world of nervous tension, aggression, and competition. The blue-collar man was protected from all that and
only had to confront boredom.

As our white-collar man goes on, he gradually realizes that he
has become a permanent contestant at the Olympics. Only the
Olympics are of short duration and all the contestants are
champions to begin with. The world of work, by contrast, is long-
lived, and most of the contestants, including our young man, are

of very average ability. Nevertheless, his company is being run as
though every worker were a champion. So is the whole economy,
which is geared to the performance capacities of its Olympians,
rather than to those of normal people.

Myron Brenton has pointed out that jobs are rated in terms of
prestige. As a consequence, about 80% of the men comprising the
work force are failures because the jobs they perform are sub-
Olympian in status. No woman has been defined as a failure to
start with, by rating her on her wife and mother capacities, not
her Olympian worker capacities. But even the 20% of men who
wear the mantle of glory cannot afford to relax, because prestige
wears out and must be constantly renewed.

When Adam Smith first tutored the world in the desirability of
turning the work world into a permanent Olympics, it never occurred to him that most men were not champions and that the
rules that produced excellence in sports competitions might produce chaos among mere mortals, who desired simply to get their
bread with as little fuss and bother as possible. Nor did he foresee
the possibility that technology might demote ordinary man into
a subordinary cog in a machine.

For that matter, his greatest blunder was the failure to see
that, in view of the genetic load of aggression carried by the male,
putting man into a competitive system was like giving a boy a
loaded gun. It wasn't as though Adam Smith didn't know about
male aggression. His society did not use the term *aggression,* but
it had another—*evil*—which meant the same thing in a religious
context. Smith's church was constantly pointing out to him man's
capacity for evil. This same church had gone to extraordinary
efforts to contain man's aggressiveness and greed by forbidding
most practices we take for granted today, especially lending
money at interest.

But Adam Smith and his school of thought redefined greed as
materialism, and pronounced it a great good. Thus, man's aggression was not only freed from restraint, but elevated to the
status of his highest virtue, and we have been paying for it ever
since. The world of competition didn't just happen to grow, like
Topsy; competition was unleashed as a social force by the system-
atic destruction of all the protective, cooperative institutions that
had characterized the feudal world. In the feudal world no one
starved, unless there was a general crop failure or a dominant
figure failed in his duty toward his subordinates. But the *threat*
of starvation was needed as a motor force in a competitive system.
Therefore, the need was turned into a reality by abolishing the

poor laws which granted charitable relief to the starving. One of the advances of modern times was to make it possible for people to starve because they didn't have work. Many promptly took advantage of this social "improvement" by doing just that—starving.

By putting a premium on aggression, the most aggressive, of course, got to the top of Mount Olympus. In free-enterprise thought, this process is both normal and desirable. But in terms of our more modern understanding, it was putting the worst at the top. As the champions accumulated at the top, they more and more changed the rules of society into Olympic rules, and forced ever more competitive rules on those who didn't wish to compete at all.

The thought that we might have put the governance of the world into the hands of our emotional cripples, rather than into those of our most humane men, is no more digestible to us today than it was to Adam Smith. Yet it is no secret, and documented by more than one study, that our leaders in the economic world are driven men—men with a compulsion to work, men for whom work is a refuge from other problems. Smith saw competition as bracing or stimulating—it never occurred to him it could be savage or ulcerating, and lead to a condition of permanent crisis. He believed that a bracing competition would simply drive prices down to their lowest point. He failed to foresee that extreme competition would drive prices even lower than that. He stood aloof from such problems because he was a professor and therefore a member of the leisured, consuming class. The harm of low prices was felt by the worker.

Because the leisured, consumer class was so small, he underplayed the difference between worker and consumer. But when the leisure class expanded beyond the narrow band of aristocracy the distinction became important, in theory as well as in fact. The consumer became a hypothetical creature distinct from the worker, and this distinction remained valid until the 20th-century, when the worker himself became a consumer. At that point it became invalid, although economists continued to use it. When both the worker and the consumer were the same person, a competition that was bad for the worker part of the person was good for his consumer part and vice versa.

But an overly competitive world was interested only in the consumer, and allowed itself to develop in ways which were bad for the worker. A world in which a balance is to be struck between competitive and cooperative forces, will be a world which will recognize that the consumer and the worker are two faces, two halves of the same person, and will put these two halves together. It will be a world aimed at the good of the whole person, not of a part. Competition is a centripetal force, which makes things fly apart. Cooperation is a centrifugal force, which pulls things together at the center. Each force must be balanced against the other, or the machine either explodes or implodes.

Yet, as the devil is more at home in hell, certain creatures are more at home in the economically centripetal world than they would be in a balanced system. There are natural champions who think it desirable to run the world on the principles of Olympic competition rather than on principles conducive to the well-being of the majority of natural losers. The natural champion Eddie Rickenbacker is one. An inheritor of wealth like William F. Buckley, Jr., also a natural champion, is another. To one who has it made, any change is a change for the worse, because there is only one way to go for those on the top—down. To the natural champions and the wealthy we must add that minority of economic conservatives, thinkers like Milton Friedman, who, protected from the rigors of competition by academic tenure and never exposed to the bracing winds of competition, never catch pneumonia and die.

By everyone else, especially those who have experienced competition, it is cordially detested. Those who don't know they detest it demonstrate their unconscious aversion by the ingenuity with which they avoid it, and the frantic way in which they hunt for security. Competition is a medicine which seems always to be recommended for other people's ailments; it is never a remedy one prescribes for oneself. Adam Smith and John Stuart Mill arrived at their philosophical positions purely on the basis of cogitation, not via the experience of competing. Thus, they failed to be aware of the limited capacities of the human nervous system, which is programmed for neat, circumscribed crises, not for perpetual ones.

Yet, having built up momentum for three centuries, it is not surprising that the competitive system knocks down every obstacle in its path and rolls on unabated, providing aggression with every possible opportunity for legitimized expression. No one seems to know how to get the genie back into the bottle. Once created, these impersonal market forces that govern us all are much more effective than personified villains at keeping us all in subjection.

Nevertheless, though resistance is theoretically impossible, and war has not been formally declared, this system is under vigorous attack. Guerilla strikes and sabotage are endemic. All classes are in revolt against it, not just the intellectuals. But because most of the guerillas are operating independently from one another, in isolation rather than in organization, the state of war is not recognized as such. Great masses of the warriors are even unconscious of the fact that they are in revolt, and do not relate their private aversion to the system to the actions of the overt rebels. They go so far as to expressly repudiate those who are in open revolt, little knowing that they are brothers.

How people resist the system depends largely on where they find themselves within it. Location controls the style of reaction. Intellectuals are soldiers making a frontal, external, attack. Blue-collar and office workers, are for the most part fifth columnists, working as sappers. Many confine themselves to passive resistance. Still others do not fit into this schema at all.

At the present stage of history, we have two, distinct economies, plus a considerable number of individuals who are part of neither. The big economy, the one Galbraith draws our attention to, is the dominant modern one of the huge conglomerates making products for which demand is, or is made to be, *inelastic*. People keep buying them no matter how high the price goes. In the other, subordinate economy, demand is *elastic*. People buy less as the prices rises. In this antique economy, the firms are small, numerous, and entirely at the caprice of the market place. They cannot rig the price of their product. That is set by the marketplace. In this old-fashioned economy, profits are low or nonexistent, and the pay is concomitantly poor. People are in it because they can't get out. In the big economy, profits are enormous and the pay is good. For example, cigarette manufacturers are in the big economy where prices are set. At this writing, they pay $2.51 per hour. Cigar manufacturers, by contrast, are part of the old-fashioned economy. Profits are miserable, and the pay is $1.39.

Galbraith maintains that the big economy is a secure one, but you could never tell it from the way the workers in it act, nor from the incidence of ulcers among them. The higher-ups live in the world of Machiavelli; the lower echelons get their dose of competition in terms of "grades" and status competition. While it is true that prices and market shares in the big economy are relatively stable, competition still makes itself uncomfortably felt. These corporations stake everything on new product development. They rarely lose, but the risk is so great that the fear factor remains enormous. Competition between worker and worker is unbelievably intense in these organizations, though camouflaged by false geniality and cradle-to-grave security.

In the old-fashioned economy, the worker feels all the pressures of his opposite number in the big economy, plus the pressures of not having cradle-to-grave security and not having enough money to keep up with the Joneses. Whichever economy the worker has hitched his wagon to, the results on the nervous system are about the same. Only the methods of reacting vary.

The obviously political intellectuals from the upper middle class, overtly revolting against the establishment over the Vietnam War and the university's involvements with the military-industrial complex, are but a small part of the action—possibly the least significant part, even though the most noted. As long as these intellectuals felt that they could avoid the anomie of the commercial world by embarking upon academic or governmental careers, they were fellow-travelers of the system. But once it became obvious that the university had been captured by the marketplace and no longer served as a sanctuary for intellectuals, they became warriors in the noble cause. With the war's end, the termination of the draft, and the separation of the reformed university from the industrial world, they may become fellow-travelers again.

Fortunately, the actual numbers of students engaged in revolt is far larger than those manning the barricades for the moment. They may prove more durable. Since the mid-fifties it has been causing concern among the cognoscenti that intellectuals were avoiding the marketplace in large numbers, and opting for the groves of academe and government. An early Harvard study showed the appalling figure of something like eight out of ten graduates heading anywhere but business. A recent study by Edward Shils of the University of Pennsylvania's Wharton School of Finance revealed that even business school graduates were avoiding "business" jobs with conventional firms that took a narrow view of business, and were hiring on with "socially conscious" firms that were aware of their responsibility to the public. This new type of young business man is symbolically copping out of the conventional competitive system and opting for a new cooperative style of business firm. That he is not a radical is demonstrated by the fact that such a young man with an M.B.A. commands a starting salary of $12,000 per year.

In his aforementioned book, *The Organization Man,* William Whyte came to the conclusion that the only way an individual, wishing to work in the white-collar world, could meet the impossible demands of business, was by cheating. He so advised his readers, with regard to the depth interviews and other probing profile devices cooked up by psychologists for ambiguous purposes. He counseled the job seeker to tell the personnel man what he wanted to hear.

Having once worked in a firm that sold these services to personnel men, and witnessed the way in which individuals were disqualified from jobs on the basis of glib opinions by psychologists I wouldn't trust to read the time correctly, I heartily second the motion, although my support is no longer needed. These tests were completely unvalidated, and may have had no more truth value than a Ouija board. Yet I saw hundreds of men barred from jobs by decisions based on the alleged expertise of men who might not have been able to hold a candle to the rejected applicant.

Competition today is so virulent in universities that cheating is looked upon as a normal part of academic life. Not to cheat in a dishonest system is regraded by students as the height of ingenuousness. Even strongholds of the honor system, like West Point and the Air Force Academy, have buckled as numbers of cadets have cooperated in organized cheating to keep up with the demands of the establishment. But when cheating becomes wholesale, we must question the legitimacy of the system that produces it.

Stress is not being experienced by the sensitive intellectual alone. Nervous breakdown, random violence (not connected to racial tension), suicide, alcoholism, homosexuality, and desertion, are increasing at a startling rate. Even after scaling down the figures to adjust for other causes, there is no alternative to the interpretation that disaffection is widespread. Add to the above the growing problem of employee theft, malingering, expense account cheating, and restriction of output, and it is difficult to come to any other conclusion than that private sabotage is wholesale. The depredations of the TV repairman, washing machine maintenance man, and auto mechanic defy any other interpretation than that they simply think the system is corrupt, and only a fool would restrain himself when the big shots are grabbing with both hands. The lack of sexual harmony between the sexes is only one of many symptoms of a basic social malaise on a grand scale.

Trained observers see a significant increase in male passivity. The male, like the female, is beginning to shrink from the outside world. Vance Packard states that the psychotherapists he has interviewed have noted an increase in the number of passive, dependent males among their patients. Brenton's interviews with the same type of specialists corroborate that fact and go further. Some of his contacts reported that they were beginning to see an increasing number of men who envied the housewife role. These men envied the fact that women don't have to enter the rat race. The Family Service Agency of one California County told Brenton that a number of its male clients would actually like to reverse roles with their wives, to stay home while the wives go to work.

Of course, dissatisfaction with the role of breadwinner also finds simpler expression. Betty Friedan admits that "divorce in America in almost every instance sought by the husband, even if the wife ostensibly gets it." She sees in this phenomenon "a growing aversion and hostility that men have for the feminine millstone around their necks."

Those who think the stress of modern living is being exaggerated, need only look at the younger generation. It is copping out in all directions, but mostly in the directions of revolution, crime, and drugs. When all the rationalizations have been made, it is patently obvious that the whole drug scene is no more than an avenue of escape from a reality too painful for many youths to bear. The very jargon of the movement makes this manifest—to "take a trip," "tune in," "turn on," "drop out," etc. Its adherents are by no means all weaklings looking for crutches. Many of these young people taking drugs are competing effectively, and holding their own. But even they find reality something from which one must retreat periodically.

Th involvement in crime on the part of youngsters for whom disadvantaged environment is not an excuse, is staggering. In middle-class surburban areas, such involvement of children under the age of eighteen is actually higher than the national average. Almost one half of all serious crimes—murder, rape, robbery, aggravated assault, burglary, larceny, and auto theft—are committed by youths under 18! Permissive upbringing is only one of several contributing factors. The principal cause is that social unrest has triggered aggression in these youths, and they take out their hostilities on the older generation through crime. The knowledge that they can get away with it, simply makes them more cocky.

Add to those who are copping out through drugs and crime, those who are expressing their hostility overtly by direct political action—the revolutionaries, who amount to about 5-10% of college youth—and we have a considerable amount of revenge being triggered by our American way of life. Every generation has had its rebels, but this generation is not just a repetition of former ones. They are not simply acting out Oedipus complexes, though that is surely one element in their rebellion. Above and beyond that, this generation is genuinely convinced that our system is brutal and unjust, and must either be stopped or beaten at its own game.

Perhaps the most significant reaction to the system is to be found not among drug addicts, criminals, or political activists, but among the young who have not lost their grip. There is an important segment of youth who are voting with their feet, and simply leaving the system. This group is genuinely trying to find another way of life. Their efforts are persistent, and they are not deterred by failure and obstacles.

First they attempted to create their own neighborhoods in the cities, like any other minority groups. When the influx of tourists ruined this and sent rents sky-high, they tried moving out to rural areas and taking over farms. The communistic and group-sex aspects of some of these groups—over-reported, as usual—have labeled them as simply Bohemian settlements. Some of them *are* simply that, but many of them are more. I have personally seen some of these young people, leading square and conventional lives in these rural areas, trying hard to make a living. They are hampered by being unaccustomed to hard labor and often by an excessive amount of human decency; but they are willing to work, and they work hard. They are genuinely engaged in a Thoreauean attempt to simplify life by going back to the land. Whether they will succeed on their own terms or only as symbols of a new attitude, is not foreseeable.

The significance of their effort is that never before in American history have such large numbers of the young walked out on the establishment in repudiation of it. Previous Utopian experiments have always involved a handful of adults. This crop consists of a mass of youth.

No statistical studies are available on the numbers involved in retreat into drugs, or in retreat to the land, though some are available for the political fighters. But one thing is clear: This is not just another generational fling; we are witnessing nothing less than an historic transformation.

Even the establishment squares are rebelling—in their way. A successful advertising executive openly admitted that the big money in advertising came not from economically important products but from items such as soaps and deodorants. "If they didn't advertise at all," he said, "it wouldn't make very much difference to anybody." But they do advertise, and determine the flow of ideas coming over TV, out of proportion to their worth. Newspapers live or die, not according to whether their readers like them, but according to whether their advertisers like them.

Even the personnel men are finally getting the word. The Industrial Relations Center of California Technological Institute discovered that the men in middle management—the most vital strata—having had enough aggression to claw their way three-fourths up the ladder, don't like the view and regress into goof-off patterns. They are no longer willing to take on new tasks; they start exercising the perquisites of office in little ways, like coming in late and leaving early, in addition to taking long lunch hours. Generally, though this group is still young, loss of aggression among its members is marked. When the "middle manager" gets an opportunity to bail out completely via an offer from government or the academic establishment, he is quite likely to grab it. Turnover thus occurs where the firm can least afford it.

Not all women pursuing careers have been blinded by neo-feminist theory and propaganda. Many—careerists and stay-at-homes—are well aware that the work world is not a glamorous and exciting place. This is how Suzanne Barrett, a journalist on my local newspaper, describes a typical day in the "glamorous" life of a career man in the executive world: "He catches a train at 7:10 to spend over an hour getting to the city. Then he will fight his way into Wall Street without getting a wrinkle. That's a lot of laughs. . . . He spends hours sitting in drafty terminals . . . or on excitingly late jets. . . . He will eat the same menu (at the same annual dinner and give the same speech to the same men who later talk about the same thing in the same bar in the same hotel) . . . he will get the same pain in the stomach later. Howls. His ideas are stolen or ravaged beyond recognition, and he lives with a promotion-happy underling, but he doesn't dare leave an impossible situation because he is over 40. Screams. . . ."

Miss Barrett may or may not have known that in addition to everything else, this over-40 executive may have been overqualified for his job in the first place. In a shortsighted effort to get the best man the salary will buy, the personnel department raised educational requirements beyond the level which the job assignment actually required. The practice of demanding more education than the job requires has become more and more widespread since the movement first began in the 1920's. The original time-and-motion man, Frederick Taylor, discovered this fact fifty years ago; in the next generation of personnel men, A. J. Snow, then a psychologist at Northwestern University, discovered it again. It has made no dent whatever in the thinking of upper management. In the 1960's Ivan Berg rediscovered it independently for the third time.

How big business can complain about corporate taxes on the one hand and persistently follow practices that raise taxes unnecessarily on the other, is a matter for wonderment. What this practice has done to the tax rates is anybody's guess. What it has meant in further suffocation of the individual male is obvious. And what it has done to the companies' immediate internal costs, as well as long-term costs, is well documented. The overeducated worker gets bored faster, quits more readily, and creates a higher turnover cost than the less educated one. Perhaps most invidious of all is the further entrenchment of the widespread belief that all learning must take place in a classroom and be duly certificated. Thinking people know that this system of classroom processing, which is the most effective way to teach large numbers of children, is the most inefficient and costly way of teaching adults!

There are some signs that the dinosaur is beginning to learn, and that the rigid, formal hierarchy, which so heavily penalizes masculinity, is on the way out. In 1965 Warren Bennis predicted that the "pyramidal, centralized, functionally specialized, impersonal mechanism, known as bureaucracy," was out of joint with the times and destined to disappear during the next twenty-five to fifty years. Four years later, writing in *TransAction,* he admitted that his forecast had been in error by some twenty years. The new organizational form he had predicted, the "task force," had already surfaced in the aerospace, drug, construction, and consulting industries. Others concur.

Dr. Newton Margulies of the Graduate School of Administration at the University of California, conducted the following experiment in a business in that state. Two departments were experimentally reorganized so as to operate on the group cooperation, or task force, principle. By comparison to the rest of the departments, which continued to operate in the old hierarchical way, workers in the experimental departments scored significantly higher on tests of self-actualization. Since this is crucial to job satisfaction, Dr. Margulies concluded that the traditional authority hierarchy may be an inefficient system of organization.

What will come of these ideas cannot be speculated on here. I merely wish to show that the problem is not hopeless, and that change is in the making.

All signs of resistance and incipient change point to one conclusion: Technological change in our overwrought competitive system has reached a velocity no longer tolerable to an increasing number of people—especially the younger generation. They have not had a chance to grow with it but have to face it all at once, and it frightens them. Aggression, as expressed through competition, has created unbearable tension, and the nervous breaking point has been reached. There is no possibility for our economic-social system to develop further along its present trajectory, without breaking down the society of which it is supposed to be only a subordinate part.

Sabotage of the system is already significant, rebellion against it is widespread, and desertion is rampant. Any army that suffered this much sabotage, rebellion, and desertion, would quit the field. But the failure of our political generals to get the point is not just a case of malfunctioning intelligence apparatus. It is due to the fact that they are old minds in a new world. From one point of view, our crisis is caused as much by massive obsolescence at the top as by anything else. Never have so many been so incompetent in the face of great historical challenge.

But it should be stated, for what it is worth, that the breaking point is not an absolute one. What is intolerable for the younger generation has been taken in stride by the older one. And what the present older generation complained about in its youth was a mere nothing to its parent generation. The fact is that, generation by generation, tension increases, while the capacity to take it decreases.

The rise of Western civilization was predicated upon the development of a colossal self-discipline and self-denial which was absolutely novel in man. Each generation coming up, being a little freer from the grim necessity that originally stimulated this iron discipline, loses some of that discipline. Each generation grows up a little more playful, a little more spontaneous, a little more fantasy oriented. It is oriented around taking, not giving, toward consuming, not producing, toward playing, not working.

The present older generation, which shaped itself during the rigors of the Depression, had only a mild dose of consumeritis. The males easily made the switch to the worker orientation when they grew up. But the present younger generation has grown up almost completely consumer-oriented. The males are experiencing extraordinary difficulty in making the switch to a worker orientation. The malignancy of the system, plus the reduced ability of the males to adapt to it, make the crisis more severe than it has ever been before.

As this process of disciplinary letdown continues generation after generation, there will obviously come a generation which cannot make the switch at all. This one now rebelling may be the one.

The progressive relaxation of tension results in a race between automation and the complete loss of the self-discipline imposed by the fear of starvation. If automation can present us with a push-button world before the last shred of discipline is lost, and the work of the future can be done in a creative, playful mood, no harm will have been done. But if all discipline is lost before automation has delivered that push-button world, we are in for another Decline and Fall.

As the letdown progresses, all kinds of work become objectionable—except *creative* work. This is particularly true of muscular work. Blue-collar work is avoided, not only because of its low prestige value but because it is disliked in itself. We have rapidly evolved into an order of men who take no joy in exertion. Yet the use of muscle is of the essence of the masculine experience, sex being the other half of that essence. Sex is more basic than work, and one can become masculine simply by experiencing sexual intercourse with a woman. But the muscle is available to the boy far earlier than the penis, and without the attendant complications. Through his muscles, the boy can be introduced to a genuine, self-validating, masculine experience. The paucity of such opportunities in male life ought to suggest to us that we cherish the few that are left.

The last generation of men who took joy in the use of their muscles, and learned to be masculine through exertion, is dying out. These were the men who were adolescents during World War I and young bucks during the twenties. This was the last generation for whom hard, muscular labor was an almost mystical experience, leading to both exultation and inner peace (as well as to coarseness and early death). It is the last generation that knew in its bones, not just in its cortex, that work, not husband-hood, was the central experience for man. These men did not work in order to support women and children; family support was a by-product of their work. It is an indication of the swift-ness of change in our time that what was so recently a source of pride and contentment is now a source of distaste. And yet work is infinitely superior to drugs as a source of identity.

We may or may not make the change from compelled work to creative work without a ripple. That is for the future to tell. Right now we are experiencing a gap between what the system demands—and what the older generation gave—and what the younger generation is willing and able to give.

In sum, the changes that took place in the economic system when labor left the home for the office and factory, have placed a debit in the masculine account, not compensated for by matching credits. The economic system demands from him total support of, and responsibility for, his wife and children. This is unique in history. It also demands of him a femininity likewise unique in history. There has always been a hierarchy in which the mass of men were subordinate to a few. But never before has society been so unrelenting regarding both the quantity and the quality of his submission.

The chief evidence for the pervasiveness of this enforced femininity is man's depressed sexuality. Feminine values, plus the feminine behavior demanded by the economic system, have crippled men. Both stimuli are working against the biological grain. Man was made to be dominant, but everywhere we see him subordinate. Biology inclines him toward masculinity, but the social forces of our time want to feminize him. He has good reason to resist these forces; they show themselves to be linked to widespread neurosis in women and permanent crisis in the society at large.

Here we run into an apparent contradiction: True—women and work tend to push man into perpetual crisis. But is not that precisely what he was made for? Did we not describe his uniqueness as lying in his crisis-facing apparatus?

The answer is "yes, but——." Man was made to face crisis, but a *hunting* crisis of short duration. The crisis he finds himself in now is not only long; it is chronic.

We know that crisis triggers the adrenal glands to release into the bloodstream certain secretions which make available extra reserves of energy. But these secretions were meant to be emergency reserves only. If the crisis is not resolved, the body chemistry is reversed and the body will eventually go into shock. Those secretions which are credits in the short run, are debits in the long run. Either we change the perpetual crisis nature of our economic system, or man will collapse.

In Part I of this book I have outlined the general ethological, genetic, endocrinological, and psychological reasons for man's dominance over women. In Part II, I endeavored to show how this long-term program has been upset by the short-term forces acting on man at the present time. We have seen that they are in conflict, and that this conflict demands early resolution.

In sketching both these forces, I have touched superficially on a number of themes that in themselves demand more profound treatment. Such treatment in depth is available elsewhere. I have restricted myself to limning only those forces which directly affect the power relation between man and woman. And I have chosen to give my main themes precedence over details, because overall concepts are, at this juncture of history, more important than reiteration of the details they rest upon.

It is now time to prescribe the solution to the problems of woman's neurosis, man's oppression, and the imbalance of the emotional economy. If my description has been accurate, the prescription for any part is the same as the prescription for the whole.

Conclusion

Now that we have placed the problem of women into the context of the total emotional economy, we are in a position to judge the feminist demands. We can see that both sexes have been subjected to the distorting pressures of the new technology; the twists in the personality structure of each can now be seen to be functionally complementary, rather than being random developments. When technology took work out of the home it split the family and threw the burdens of two onto the shoulders of one. As a result, men became overtaxed and women underchallenged. The problem is easily solved on the theoretical level by simply redistributing the burden.

Awareness of the simplicity of the problem and its solution was delayed by the feminist leadership's failure to distinguish between the two ways in which women relate to men in the modern world —through subordination, and through dependency. This failure led to an oversimplified, one-part solution to a two-part problem. Women summed up their whole case in a demand for equality— which was only half a solution. They felt that they would be all right once they obtained a parity of privilege, or right, with men, and failed to note that a parity of privilege is not synonymous with a parity of power. They failed to see that after the struggle for equality produced those structural reforms which made approximate equality possible, they would still remain socially unequal because of their economic dependency. This could only be changed by a reach for parity of power through the assumption of responsibility for self-support. They did not see that while political equality can be demanded and given, independence cannot be given but must be taken. Feminine intuition was right in perceiving something radically wrong in the relations between the sexes. Men were so riveted to the survival problem that they never would have seen this by themselves.

But upon this solid foundation of intuition the feminists erected a rickety superstructure of thought and wasted much of their effort. So deeply imbued were they with the notion that men had to support them, that they never sensed the incongruity between this notion and the demand for full equality. It never occurred to many women that men's superior social position was bought and paid for by performance; in a way, this blind spot constitutes a tribute to how well men have done their job of creating a sheltered place for women to live in.

The movement to assume responsibility, chiefly through work and self-support, should have been Part II of the feminist program. But through vague thinking, and a distaste for responsibility—partly caused by a lesser endowment of aggressiveness—the distaff side made only a feeble, halfhearted stab at work.

This half of a solution was, in effect, even less than half, because women did not understand that their lack of aggression made perfect equality in any sphere impossible. In their private, intimate life, there was no hope of it. In their public life, in the world of work and affairs, radical improvements in their status could be made, but their lack of gameness would still make them second-placers. Even in civilized society some things can only be obtained by fighting for them. Equality is one of these things. Yet women kept demanding a full equality which they could neither earn nor fight for or, for that matter, hold on to, if it had been possible to give it. At the same time they failed to take the practical steps which could give them some power, and earn them the respect of men.

They continued to rely on shrill rhetoric rather than deeds. The entire question of the place of women in society has therefore always been obscured by a miasma of shrewishness, which made feminist demands seem phony. In terms of their strength and ability to hold a position, men knew intuitively that women weren't worth what they demanded. But they could not communicate to women why their demands were excessive, so women continued to view male resistance as injustice. Men understood in their bones that society had to be a patriarchy. Women, to achieve a place in the sun, seemed to want to destroy that patriarchy, aiming at something neutral, equating social justice with sexual neuterness. Believing as they did, men failed to see that special arrangements had to be made within the patriarchy, so that women could function as human beings. And feminists failed to see that they had to make room for themselves within the partiarchy without destroying it.

Thus, after a full generation of pause, when the feminists moved to clean up the unfinished business of their sex, they unimaginatively ran up the old banner of equality and the related slogans of Phase I, rather than the banner and slogan appropriate for Phase II—independence. They still hadn't learned the difference.

Under the new historical circumstances, this failure of feminine intuition had become dangerous, not just inept. The burden of feminine dependence had grown much worse during the long armistice. True, a portion of the female sex had gone to work, but not nearly enough of them did and men were still legally responsible for the maintenance of their wives. In consequence, the renewed call for ever more equality looked like an increase in parasitism. Totally unaware that they might produce just the opposite result from what they intended, the new feminists marched on, aroused by the discovery of still existing pockets of structural inequality, and blind to the observation that the very triviality of these remnants was an indication that the battle was over. The bastion had already been taken.

Yet, though some support accrued to the cause from the young, the majority of women with some experience of life did not respond as they had once before. In fact, many women were antagonized. These women were eminently satisfied with a well-upholstered dependency, and did not like to see it jeopardized. Less aggressive and ambitious than their champions, they did not want to work and wished the leadership would carry the banner without dragging in the rest of them. The new feminists were not speaking for the majority.

However, their minority of support included some men of the academic community, especially among the ranks of social scientists. Within this community, opposition to any democratic demand was equivalent to heresy. It was from this group that recommendations emanated, hinting that modifications of masculine attitudes were in order, to accomodate the realities of the contemporary world.

But these men supported feminism because they thought feminine inequality stemmed from arbitrary cultural styles. They failed to recognize the innate, hereditary component to subordination which made the call for social justice irrelevant. Once they understand the role of aggression in male dominance, their support will vanish.

We now know that feminine subordination is not a real problem, because the female is programmed for it in a way that defies tinkering. At the same time we now understand that cultural circumstances have thrown women into an historically unnatural total dependence, for which they were not programmed. With these cultural circumstances we are free to tinker to our heart's content.

The confusion between subordination and dependency, and the definition of the feminist goal of equality, inevitably led the feminists into political agitation. The redefinition of their problem as one of excessive dependency will also inevitably redirect these efforts towards their proper goal—a job. Women need not keep demanding that which they already have in substance—legal rights. They should start exercising them. But woman's lack of aggression will make it mandatory for man to help her redirect her efforts, as she has shown an inability to do this for herself.

Upon mature consideration of the biological evidence, discerning men must reject feminist demands *in their present form*. With respect to the masculine-feminine realtionship, men need make no significant changes in their behavior—beyond hardening their attitude. To advise men to treat women as equals now, while they are essentially in a parasitical relationship, is to advise men to acquiesce to and legitimize conditions which are crippling to both sexes. It is also to ask men to do the impossible. No one who is dependent can be other than a subordinate. To be equal, one must be independent; to be approximately equal one must be approximately independent.

What we need to do now, is not to attempt to gerrymander the definition of masculinity to fit into distorted conditions, but to straighten out the distortions. We must correct warped feminine values, and crippling conditions of work.

On the basis of historical evidence the first should be easy to do, since it requires only a period of enlightenment. The second should be impossible, since it implies controlling the uncontrollable, but it is being done anyway.

The concept of masculinity has never before been subject to such a direct challenge. The concept has millions of years of biological respectability behind it, while the challenge is no more than a hundred years old. From the evolutionary point of view, it is premature to find masculinity wanting. Women's challenge to it stems from their neurosis; the challenge from technology results from short-term maladaptation of technology. There is nothing premanently inevitable about either feminine conditions of work or feminine values. Neither are healthy and therefore neither are durable. Nor can the male nervous system tolerate either of them permanently. There is something intrinsically suspicious in the idea of an able-bodied half of a superior species being totally dependent upon the other half. Dependency is for the young, the old, the sick, the indigent, and the temporaily out-of-luck, not for the healthy.

The adjustments that need to be made in our system, must be made by women, and by the system itself. It is not men who are out of step with the system or with women; it is women and the system that are out of step with men. True, our species may be endangered by excessively stimulated aggression, but it has not outgrown the need for aggressiveness, initiative, and guts. Nor is technology likely to make these characteristics obsolete. They will remain top-priority characteristics for man, as long as they are effectively disconnected from war. A day will come when this planet will burn out. But long before that happens, it will be subjected to repeated disasters on a global and galactic scale. Our kind will not survive these disasters, or be safely transplanted to another part of the universe, by feminized men or falsely inflated women. It will take fully masculine men to accomplish that feat. The present effort to phase out masculinity is well intended, but misdirected. It is the present epoch which must itself be phased out.

The price of women has never been so astronomically high. Man is at his masculine nadir now. There has been a steady decline in his authority and status, with concomitant increase in responsibilities. At the present time, the only indisputable right left him is the right to pay. No wife, son, or daughter challenges that right; nor have they voluntarily taken upon themselves responsibilities equal to the new freedoms that have fallen to them. The emotional economy is unstable, and will have to move definitely in one direction or another to achieve a new equilibrium. If male responsibility is to remain at its present high level, wife and children will have to retreat to a traditional attitude of deference. But this would not straighten out the distortions.

A better equilibrium could be established by shifting some of the excess male responsibility to wife and children—though neither can be expected to cooperate in the transfer. The male should abdicate the exquisite pleasure of paying for the play of others, and the right to be ridiculed and held up to contempt while he is doing it. He should adopt a more consumer-like attitude towards his family, and value them in proportion to the satisfactions they bring him.

Woman rationalizes her retreat from reality by indicting man as the obstacle to her growth. He once was, and a minority still is. But the real villain of the piece is woman herself, and her own lack of fortitude. When she meets an obstacle—the very same one met by man—she reacts with a sense of surprised outrage. The obstacle wasn't supposed to be there. That the path is obstructed is "unfair," and punishment must be meted out. She finds a culprit: it is man who is barring her path.

But the fact that women no longer know that obstacles are natural, is in itself an indication of how depreciated they are. The knowledge of the naturalness of obstacles is one of the most elementary perceptions a person can have. To be petulantly surprised by them is the response of the immature, and it is alarming that one half of the species must have spelled out to it a fact which is central to its existence.

The subordinate-dependent relationship of woman to man, created by modern technology, is one always open to degeneration into parasitism. Recent generations have not only so degenerated but have tended to institutionalize that degeneration, to the extent that it is now regarded as normal. In teaching boys, women have corrupted the principle that men must work into the self-serving principle that men must support women. This slight skew has hidden a massive dislocation in the emotional economy. These duties are neither synonymous nor equal in weight: The greater duty is for men to work; the lesser duty by far is to support women.

Man's important effort is to himself and to his kind, not just to his womenkind. There are canals to be built, planets to be explored, beans to be canned, and poems to be written, none of this for the special benefit of women. The work of the world is unlimited, and man's duty to it is unlimited. Man's duty towards women *is* limited, and balances woman's limited duty towards man.

Those women who doubt that there has been an imbalance in responsibilities between the two sexes might manipulate the arguments for themselves, and weigh the conclusions. For example, since equality means equal responsibilities as well as equal rights, can women refuse to do heavy and dirty work simply because they are weak? Have they any more right to refuse garbage collecting than the muscularly weak male? Should not equal women serve equally as combat troops in war? They have before, but would they consent to do so always?

To ask these questions is to see the flaw in the equality concept. Woman will not match man dirty job for dirty job. Therefore she cannot be equal to him. The more responsibility woman rejects, the more unequal she makes herself.

Women have traditionally avoided this argument about dirty work and war by pointing out that, while they cannot match men in dirty work, neither can men match them in having babies. If having a baby were as risky to life as waging war, women would have a valid point. But it no longer is. Yet the claim persists because women have lost contact with the reality of the survival problem as it is experienced in work. It is also perpetuated by the suspicion that because women have missed out on sexual frolic they probably have missed out on many other goodies. To these sources of support for a myth of equal contribution, yet another one must be added: The demand for equality also stems from the play orientation children are now reared in, as opposed to the old work orientation. Play is spontaneous and unfettered, without discipline. It also stimulates a resentment against any kind of imposed restriction. But women remain in what are essentially play orientations, long after play time is over and men have been called to work.

My diagnosis will not be eagerly embraced by women. It is fairly unpalatable and likely to be ignored. Neo-feminist agitation will continue because it provides a rationalization for deprivation. But I am not standing out against a general criticism of the establishment. I agree with those who consider it fossilized and in need of reform. I simply do not agree with the particular reform of equality for women, as long as it continues to mean increased parasitism. I wholeheartedly support all moves in the direction of feminine independence.

At this moment of history, though the female still has somewhat less structual equality than the male, the difference is technical rather than substantial. She has a considerable amount of freedom. What she needs is to use it, but this is precisely what she shrinks from doing. Her inaction, or action in the wrong direction, compels the male to initiate moves that will restore the balance of the emotional economy. It is up to the prospective bridegroom to query the bride about her future work plans. It is up to the husband to ask the wife when she plans to return to work. It is up to men in general to point out to affluent men in particular, that there are other ways of demonstrating success than maintaining an idle woman in the shop window.

Though there are many women able to transfer themselves immediately from the world of the dependent to the world of the independent (and those who might secretly be relieved to do so) we must expect the change to be evolutionary rather than revolutionary. Many women and couples are too committed, psychologically and otherwise, to the world of feminine dependency to make the requisite change. The most urgent task is to prepare the young female for the world of independence; she should be reared with the expectation that she will be self-supporting for life, except for the periods of active maternity.

But in general, in the face of the persistent demands by the feminists, men should firm up their position. We should show our liberal determination to support social justice by giving women all the help they need to find and hold a job. Only when we have had at least two successive generations of self-supporting women will be be able to make an exact statement as to whether the sexes can be truly equal or not. If experience shows that women can carry as much responsibility as men, then there can be no further reason not to hold perfect equality as a democratic principle. But if women fail to match men responsibility for responsibility, that result too closes out the books on the question.

In order to put the question to the test of reality once and for all, I propose to counter the neo-feminist demand for greater freedom and equality with a masculinist demand for equal responsibility:

(1) For every human freedom, there should be an equivalent responsibility.

This is a demand of life directed at all people *as people,* not simply as members of a sex. It applies to children as well as to adults, even though, at the present historical moment, it has more applicability to women than to men or children. We have gone through a long period during which basic freedoms were articulated and proclaimed. Perhaps we are now entering an epoch during which the responsibilities that match the freedoms will be articulated and enshrined. These responsibilities can be regarded as the price of the freedoms. Those who will not pay the price cannot enjoy the freedoms.

One of the freedoms that were enunciated at great human cost was the right not to be enslaved and used for the life purposes of another. Slavery was seen to be a cultural condition imposed by man, not by biology. The historical struggle concerned itself exclusively with physical slavery, and the Emancipation Proclamation in this country concerned itself with the slavery of the body. With the perspective provided by time, slavery was seen to arise in many contents other than the strictly physical. There was social, mental, emotional, and ideological slavery as well. Discerning individuals realized that people had a right, not only to the sovereignty over their own bodies, but over their own minds and thoughts as well. As women have a right to their own bodies superior to the right of a fetus that may come to inhabit it, so do

(2) *Men have a right to be free from exploitation, a right not to be used for another's purposes, a right not to be compelled to be an unwilling host to another's dependency.*

No woman has a right to a parasitical dependence upon an unwilling male-host, except during her maternal phase. Where men choose to support women who are neither pregnant nor mothering, they do this without prejudice. That is, support should not be a legal right of the able-bodied, nonmothering wife, as it is now, but a privilege granted by the male and revocable by him at any time. The existing legal liability to support a wife is a holdover from the past. It had reference to a situation in which structural inequality was the norm. Now that structural equality is the norm, the legal obligation of men to support wives is a structural debit not balanced by any compensating credit.

This idea, translated into practice, means that women will have to go to work. They will have to work not only to earn independence in the future, but to pay for the freedoms they enjoy now. This imperative does not mean some women, some of the time, but all women all of the time. Pregnancy and childcare are to be considered merely one kind of work. When children have become comfortably adjusted to school, the woman will be expected to shift to other kinds of work.

Work, in this context, means holding down a full-time job, forty hours per week, fifty weeks per year, for forty or forty-five years of life, or whatever else the future decides to define as "work." Those women who can meet this definition can then be considered equal—or as equal as sexuality and hierarchy allow.

If man is to be truly freed from exploitation and woman from the paralysis of an ever-present option that precludes a firm commitment to some course of life, it follows that in assuming responsibility for self-support woman also assumes responsibility for her own debts, in marriage, as well as out of it. Additionally, the doctrine of "equal responsibility" implies that

> *(3) Each adult person, assumes co-responsibility, for the well-being, and the debts, of the children that issue from the marriage.*

Translated into practice, this means that a man will no longer be responsible for the debts or maintenance of his wife—or the woman with whom he cohabits—and for only half the debts of his children, except for the time during which a woman is totally employed rearing preschool children. During this period the male will be totally responsible. Thereafter, responsibility will again be shared equally; or, if husbands are to continue responsible for the debts of wives, then wives are to become responsible for the debts of husbands.

Naturally, in the world of equal rights and equal responsibilities, the travesty of alimony will be abolished. If divorce should occur during pregnacy or the preschool period, the man will still be totally responsible for all debts that accrue during that period. Once the child is safely in school, the father will revert to no responsibility for the mother and one-half, or co-responsibility, for the child. Debtor's prison for nonpayment of alimony will of course disappear, though it will continue for nonpayment of child support. But the mother will be as exposed to it as the father.

As part of the child-support question, a new legal distinction should be created. The law should catch up with modern contraceptive techniques by recognizing the phenomenon of male entrapment. That is, when in a voluntary intimacy a woman agrees to practice birth control but deliberately fails to do so and an unwanted pregnancy results, a prima facie case of entrapment exists, if the woman demands marriage.

The intent of this new distinction is clear. No man should be compelled to support a child he did not want because a woman chose to use pregnancy as a device to force marriage. Naturally, where a woman took precautions to avoid pregnancy but a truly accidental pregnancy occured nonetheless, the male will have the responsibilities of the legal father (total support for the mother and child during the years of infancy, thereafter half support for the child). Should the mother take the child out of the reach of the father, in order to accomodate the needs of a second husband or cohabitant, the father's obligations for child support should cease.

While the equal responsibility concept requires that couples should share maintenance costs, the actual division of responsibility can be left up to the individuals involved. They could share expenses equally, or in proportion to respective income. Where the man earns more he could contribute more, should he wish a standard of living higher than the one to which the woman could make an equal contribution. This would also mean that where the woman earned more she would contribute more under the same circumstances.

It is not clear exactly what effect the equal responsibility concept would have on the institution of marriage itself. It might disappear or it might continue in a modified form. The fundamental reason for legal marriage—as opposed to ceremonial or ritual marriage—as it has been handed down to us, is to protect the right of the wife and child to support and maintenance in a situation of structural inequality. But where structural equality is to be the rule, this reason for legal marriage disappears.

A portion of the younger generation appears to be already acting on this understanding by simply adopting the practice of cohabitation without legal marriage. Whether this is a harbinger of what will soon be general practice, or simply a temporary trend among a minority of individuals, only time will tell. There is much to be said for not freezing a dynamic relationship into a static legality, especially from the male's point of view. The nonlegal relationship precludes the possibility of a female acting a role in order to get a man, and dropping it once he has been captured in a legal marriage. But there is also something to be said for the traditional marriage bonds. This, however, is a subject in itself and no pronouncements upon it are really required here. The equal responsibility doctrine is compatible with either tradtional marriage or simple cohabitation.

A seemingly trivial modification in the dating practices of the young could pave the way for a smooth transition to an equal responsibility pattern. It should be made the norm for youngsters to "Dutch date." This practice will not only alter the future but is a matter of real social justice in its own right. Many young boys from poor families lead absolutely miserable lives in school because they cannot afford to date. It seems senseless for a poor boy to pay the costs of frolic for an upper-middle-class girl whose parents could well afford the expense. The doctrine of equal responsibilities for equal rights calls attention to an injustice which to many appears trivial. But in fact, the dating relation of the young boy and girl reveals much of what is wrong with the present male-female relationship.

The girl feels, "If you care for me, you'll pay for me." Money is mixed up with her self-esteem. At the same time the boy feels that having to pay for a date makes a ghoul of him—someone who is not in himself worthy of a woman's time, which he can only have by purchase.

The maladjustment between the sexes is further revealed in the fact that both are right, yet the result is wrong. If the logic is correct there must be something wrong in the premise, and there is. The error is in the accepted dependence of women. As long as that forms part of the premise, there must be conflict. To remove the conflict one must remove the dependence from the accepted premise. Once it is removed, the problem disappears. Of course, in passing, one cannot help but observe that here again we see the woman's double standard in all its dubious glory. Her wishes for equality are in one compartment of her mind; her desire for dependence in another. She is careful to keep them separate, so that no conflict arises and she can claim the best of two worlds and avoid the disadvantages of both.

As in the instance of Dutch dating, the more the doctrine of equal responsibility is studied, the more it reveals revolutionary ramifications in many spheres of life. There is nothing trivial about it.

For another example, it vitally affects the sexual sphere of life as well. One of our more unfortunate inheritances from our Puritanical past is that the male is a sexually thoughtless beast who has his brutal selfish way with a delicate girl without proper regard for her sensibilities. A corollary of this attitude is that the male is responsible for the production of the female orgasm.

Though the writers of sex manuals don't seem to know it yet, the frigid or inhibited female is largely a thing of the past. Young women today are for the most part sexually robust and lusty wenches, quite free from any suggestion of reticence or timidity in matters sexual. The female is about as healthy sexually as she can possibly be. To continue to require a man to be responsible for her orgasm is like requiring him to carry coals to Newcastle. The doctrine of equal responsibility allows us to catch up to obvious historical change and to announce that the responsibility for sexual satisfaction is now either mutual, or else individual—he is responsible for *his* orgasm and she is responsible for *hers*.

Especially should this be true when the female a man mates with may have started her sexual life conditioned to sexual pleasure by her own idiosyncrasies or those of her first lover. There is such a thing as "imprinting" in sex—the first source of true pleasure is likely to remain the permanently best source. Successor lovers are not likely to be able to compete with it, nor should they try. Admittedly, sex is an eminently cooperative venture. But if reasonable care and affection for another human being is not sufficient to lead to sexual satisfaction for the female, then she should either continue in her quest for another partner, or seek professional help. She should not lay her problems at the man's door. The sexually delicate woman is a museum piece; the modern girl can be trusted to look out for herself in this department. The doctrine of equal responsibility promises a resurgence of male spontaneity in matters sexual. It will also force a woman to come to terms with her fantasies.

The doctrine of equal responsibility calls for little effort from the male, for once; but there are some few areas in which he will have to make minor accommodations. They will be a small price to pay for the decrease in the load he has been accustomed to carry. One of the adjustments the male will have to make concerns equal pay for equal work. Though equal pay was guaranteed to women by law in 1963, it has yet to become a universal reality. But it takes little intuition to see that a woman loath to work to start with, has precious little incentive if she can earn no more than bare expenses. If she is going to pull her weight, she must be enticed with the carrot as well as beaten with the stick. If she is going to pay her own bills she must have something to pay them with.

Related to this obstacle to work is another one: The lack of nursery schools and other child care aids acts a a major deterrent to married women's working ambitions. There is no oversight more expensive to the male than this failure to provide a much needed facility, which has long been a commonplace in Europe. Current babysitter fees are prohibitive for working mothers. Between babysitting fees, transportation fees, and clothing costs, the woman frequently has little left to show for her efforts. This oversight should be remedied as soon as possible.

Also in need of remedy is the false pride that makes some men unwilling to liberate themselves from slavery. There is nothing particularly commendable or masculine about not facing reality. The fact that a man need not hold a woman through her dependency upon him, but holds her even though she does not need his support, constitutes a sufficiently valid proof of masculinity to satisfy his ego.

In general, though the masculinist shares the desire of the feminist leadership (if not the feminine rank and file) to put women to work, he does so with a radically different emphasis. The feminists urge work as a source of adventure. The masculinist already knows this to be a bit of naiveté caused by lack of exposure, and urges work as an acceptance of the doctrine of equal responsibility. He cautions the woman to expect work to be dull. If she happens to land an interesting job, the masculinist wishes her well. But whether she does or does not, he expects her to carry her half of the load.

There should be no insurmountable difficulty in the restoration of equilibrium to the emotional economy by the application of the doctrine of equal responsibility. Men need only the strength of private conviction. Each man need only make his decision not to accept feminine dependency any longer, in order to bring about a ground swell of public change. Political organization is superfluous. Time will make a *de facto* change *de jure*.

The single biggest objection to the movement of all women into the world of work is the familiar one that children will be neglected. By a caprice of the newspaper industry, this view has become the popular one even though it is erroneous. The first study of this subject brought forth the wrong result—that a working mother was harmful to the child—but it happened to be given wide publicity.

Succeeding studies which showed that not only were children not adversely affected but might even be profiting from the separation, never attracted the same kind of newspaper coverage, and so the myth continues. Patience and perseverance are the only antidotes.

This objection, when voiced by the female sex, will in fact be a cover for unwillingness. Women who prefer to work are in the minority, and men will have to be prepared for a lot of foot-dragging on the part of the other sex. Nevertheless, the outlook is far from dim.

In their eager pursuit of male privileges, women have thrown away their trump card, their immemorial hold over men. Now that they are dedicated to bigger and better orgasms, they no longer practise sexual denial as a power play. This, coupled with their greater numbers—in this country the surplus of females over males is about four million—has put the shoe on the other foot. In the generation now coming of age, young men cannot be coerced into marriage as the price of sexual satisfaction. Sex has become a free commodity. The only reasons for which a man now needs to marry are avoidance of boredom or loneliness, a desire for fatherhood, or for the sense of identity a home provides.

In the all too recent past, the possibility of having unlimited access to more than one woman, was only a fantasy for most men. Now that fantasy is a reality. The situation now facing the young man, if he will but realize it, is that a woman has to please him to get him. She must compete for him just as he used to compete for her. By reaching for equality in the sexual sphere, she has weakened her bargaining position and thrust herself further into subordination. She has, in fact, liberated men more than she has liberated herself.

Historically, those who have expatiated on the desirability of more freedom, have been immortalized. Those who have discoursed on responsibility have enjoyed little such esteem. Tom Paine is every man's hero—Edmund Burke is appreciated by only a few. The concept of responsibility is as unappetizing as the concept of freedom is popular. Responsibility is the characteristic cultures have the hardest time creating, and it is the first thing lost when change threatens. It takes long effort to break a man to harness; to be housebroken is strictly an acquired taste and one which many men never really acquire. Therefore we cannot expect to hear hymns of praise from women as we, more or less gently, push them out the door into the cold world. It will seem cruel and unjust to them, and they may curse those of their sex who have raised the issue again. But men must stand firm. Little boys benefit from the exposure, and so will little girls. The Option is a disaster, and must be banished from the realm of possibilities.

In any event, since the world of work demands submissiveness, it should not prove too uncomfortable for women. There is little difference between subordinating oneself to a boss and submitting to a lover.

As for men, we can live within a system of structural equality which will protect the fundamental rights of women—so long as it also protects men from exploitation. Within this formal structure of equality, informal inequality will prevail, as women continue to seek submission to some male in private life, while learning to live with a veneer of domination in public life. Within this structure of impersonal equality, women will have the power, not to be actually equal, but to hire and fire the boss they freely appoint to rule over themselves. Their subordination will be voluntary rather than enforced, since they will have the independence to terminate it whenever they wish. No woman will be compelled to submit to an oppressive male because the structure of society raises him and depresses her, or because she lacks the means to effect a change. Men will have comparable rights.

Neither sex will be forced to maintain a personally destructive relationship because of a warped social structure.

As women have gradually learned that they have a duty to themselves which transcends their duty to spouse and offspring, so men must also become aware that their first duty is to themselves and their own humanity. Man must be a worker, but he need not be a slave. Woman must be a temporary dependent, but she need not be a lifelong parasite. *The woman who would be perfectly equal, must be equally responsible.*

References

Introduction

Page 26 (1) de Beauvoir, Simone: *The Second Sex*. New York, Alfred A. Knopf, Inc., 1952.

Page 28 (2) Montagu, Ashley: *The Natural Superiority of Women*. New York, The Macmillan Co., 1968.

Part I.

Page 85 (1) Montagu, Ashley: Chromosomes and Crime. *Psychology Today*, October 1968, pp. 43-49.

Page 86 (2) Farber & Wilson: *The Potential of Women*. New York, McGraw-Hill Book Co., 1963.

Page 86 (3) Brenton, Myron: *The American Male: A Penetrating Look at the Masculinity Crisis*. New York, Coward-McCann, Inc., 1966.

Page 86 (4) Levy, David: *Maternal Overprotection*. New York, Columbia University Press, 1943.

Page 101 (5) Ford, Clellan S., and Beach, Frank A.: *Patterns of Sexual Behavior*. New York, Harper & Bros., 1952.

Page 108 (6) Farb, Peter: *Man's Rise to Civilization*. New York, Avon Paperbacks, 1969.

Page 110 (7) Esman, Aaron: Towards An Understanding of Racism. *Psychiat. & Soc. Sci. Rev.* 4 (Nov. 13, 1970).

Part II.

Page 121 (1) Ferguson, Charles: *The Male Attitude*. Boston, Little, Brown & Co., Inc., 1966.

Page 121 (2) Berg, Ivan: Rich Man's Qualifications for Poor Man's Jobs. *TransAction*, March, 1969.

Page 172 (3) Bennis, Warren: Post-Bureaucratic Leadership. *TransAction*, July, 1969.

Bibliography

There is a massive body of literature on the subjects of feminism, patriarchy, women's rights, etc., most of which has become obsolete within the two years preceding this book's publication. This rapid obsolescence is due to the fact that the pertinent biological discoveries concerning aggression, and their laboratory validation, have taken place within this two-year period. They have drastically changed the picture.

Therefore, to readers who come upon this book without having read some of the older ones on the subject, and who wish to sample more of the feminist viewpoint, I would recommend only the books listed below. The basic ideologies of the neo-feminists since the early 1950's are set forth in:

de Beauvoir, Simone. *The Second Sex.* New York: Alfred A. Knopf, Inc., 1952.
Friedan, Betty. *The Feminine Mystique.* New York: W. W. Norton & Co., Inc., 1963.
Montagu, Ashley. *The Natural Superiority of Women.* New York: The Macmillan Co., 1968.

Of the many books by the younger feminists, I recommend only:

Millett, Kate. *Sexual Politics.* New York: Doubleday & Co., Inc., 1969, 1970.

As a sample of male responses to the feminists I suggest:

Brenton, Myron. *The American Male: A Penetrating Look at the Masculinity Crisis.* New York: Coward-McCann, Inc., 1966.
Ferguson, Charles. *The Male Attitude.* Boston: Little, Brown & Co., 1966.
Packard, Vance. *The Sexual Wilderness.* New York: David McKay Co., Inc., 1968.

For those seeking more detailed information on the formation of the masculine and feminine personality and on the subject of aggression, the following works are recommended:

Ardrey, Robert. *African Genesis.* New York: Atheneum Publishers, 1961.
Ardrey, Robert. *The Territorial Imperative: A Personal Inquiry into the Animal Origins of Property and Nations.* New York: Atheneum Publishers, 1961.
de Vore, Irven, ed. *Primate Behavior: Field Studies of Monkeys and Apes.* New York: Holt, Rinehart and Winston, Inc., 1965.
Erikson, Erik H. *Childhood and Society.* New York: W. W. Norton & Co., Inc., 1964.
Erikson, Erik H. *Identity, Youth, and Crisis.* New York: W. W. Norton & Co., Inc., 1968.
Ford, Clellan S., and Beach, Frank A. *Patterns of Sexual Behavior.* New York: Harper & Bros., 1952.
Lorenz, Konrad. *On Aggression.* New York: Harcourt, Brace & World, Inc., 1966.
Morris, Desmond. *The Naked Apes: A Zoological Study of the Human Animal.* New York: McGraw-Hill Book Co., 1968.

204 *Bibliography*

Morris, Desmond. *The Human Zoo.* New York: McGraw-Hill Book Co., 1969.

Scott, John P. *Aggression.* Chicago: University of Chicago Press, 1958.

Stoller, Robert. *Sex and Gender: On the Development of Masculinity and Femininity.* New York: Science, 1968.

Storr, Anthony. *On Human Aggression.* New York: Atheneum Publishers, 1968.

Readers wishing to acquire a more substantial background in the genetic and endocrinological aspects of aggression are advised to turn to the scientific journals. The following list supplements the sources indicated in the References list.

Anderson, O. D. The role of the glands of internal secretion in the production of behavioral types in the dog. Section II in Stockard, C. R. The genetic and endocrine basis for differences in form and behavior. *Am. Anat. Mem.,* 1941, 19, 647-747.

Beeman, E. A. The effect of male hormone on aggressive behavior in mice. *Physiological Zoology,* 1947, 20, 373-405.

Bennett, M. A. Social hierarchy in ring doves II. The effects of treatment with testosterone propionate. *Ecology,* 1940, 21, 148-165.

Bevan, J. M., Bevan, W., and Williams, B. F. Spontaneous aggressiveness in young castrate C_3H male mice treated with three dose levels of testosterone. *Physiological Zoology,* 1958, 31, 284-288.

Bevan, W., Daves, W. F., and Levy, G. W. The relation of castration, androgen therapy and pretest fighting experience to competitive aggression in male C57BL/10 mice *Animal Behavior,* 1960, 8, 6-12.

Bevan, W., Levy, G. W., Whitehouse, J. M., and Bevan, J. M. Spontaneous aggressiveness in two strains of mice castrated and treated with one of three androgens. *Physiological Zoology,* 1958, 30, 341-349.

Bronson, F. H., and Eleftheriou, B. E. Chronic physiological effects of fighting in mice. *General and Comparative Endocrinology,* 1964, 4, 9-14.

Bronson, F. H., and Eleftheriou, B. E. Behavioral pituitary and adrenal correlates of controlled fighting (defeat) in mice. *Physiological Zoology,* 1965a, 38, 406-411.

Carpenter, C. R. Territoriality: a review of concepts and problems. In A. Roe and G. G. Simpson (eds.), *Behavior and Evolution.* New Haven: Yale University Press, 1958.

Casey, M. D., Blank, C. E., Street, D. R. K., Segall, L. J., McDougall, H. H., McGrath, P. J., and Skinner, J. L. YY chromosomes and antisocial behavior. *Lancet,* 1966b, 11, 859-860.

Chen, G., Bohner, B., and Bratton, A. C. Influence of certain central depressants on the fighting behavior of mice. *Archives Internationales de Pharmacodynamie et de Therapie,* 1963, 142, 30-34.

Cole, H. F., and Wolf, H. H. Effects of some psychotropic drugs on conditioned avoidance and aggressive behaviors. *Psychopharmacologia,* 1966, 8, 389-396.

Court Brown, W. M. Human population cytogenetics. In *Frontiers of Biology.* New York: John Wiley & Sons, Inc., 1967.

DeFries, J. C. Prenatal maternal stress in mice: Differential effects in behavior. *Journal of Heredity,* 1964, 55, 289-295.

Delgado, J. Social rank and radio-stimulated aggressiveness in monkeys. *Journal of Nervous and Mental Disease,* 1967, 144, 383-390.

DeVore, I. (ed.). *Primate Behavior.* New York: Holt, Rinehart & Winston, 1965.

Fraser, F. C., Kalter, H., Walker, B. E., and Fainstat, T. D. The experimental production of cleft palate with cortisone and other hormones. *Journal of Cellular and Comparative Physiology,* 1954, 43, 237-259.

Fredericson, E., and Birnbaum, E. A. Competitive behavior between mice with different hereditary backgrounds. *The Journal of Genetic Psychology,* 1954, 85, 271-280.

Fredericson, E., Story, A. W., Gurney, N. L., and Butterworth, K. The relationship between heredity, sex, and aggression in two inbred mouse strains. *The Journal of Genetic Psychology,* 1955, 87, 121-130.

Ginsburg, B., and Allee, W. C. Some effects of conditioning on social dominance and subordination in inbred strains of mice. *Physiological Zoology,* 1942, 35, 485-506.

Goodman, R. M., Miller, F., and North, C. Chromosomes of tall men. *Lancet,* 1968, 1, 1318.

Goodman, R. M., Smith, W. S., and Migeon, C. J. Sex chromosome abnormalities. *Nature,* 1967, 216, 942-943.

Heimburger, R. F., Whitlock, C. C., and Kalsbeck, J. E. Steriotaxic amygdalotomy for epilepsy with aggressive behavior. *Journal of the American Medical Association,* 1966, 198, 741-745.

Hunter, H. Chromatin-positive and XYY boys in approved schools. *Lancet,* 1968, 1, 816.

Ismail, A. A., Harkness, R. A., Kirkham, K. E. E., et al. Effect of abnormal sex-chromosome complements on urinary testosterone levels. *Lancet,* 1968, 1, 220-222.

Kislak, J. W., and Beach, F. A. Inhibition of aggressiveness by ovarian hormones. *Endocrinology,* 1955, 56, 684-692.

Lagerspetz, K. *Studies on the Aggressive Behavior of Mice.* Helsinki: Suomalainen Tiedeakatemia, 1964.

Levine, L., Barsel, G. E., and Diakow, C. A. Interaction of aggressive and sexual behavior in male mice. *Behaviour,* 1965, 25, 272-280.

Levine, S., and Conner, R. L. Endocrine Aspects of Violence. Report submitted to the National Commission on the Causes and Prevention of Violence, 1968.

Levy, J. B., and King, J. A. The effects of testosterone propionate on fighting behavior in young male C57BL/10 mice. *Anat. Rec.,* 1953, 117, 562-563. (Abstract)

Lindzey, G., Winston, H., and Manosevitz, M. Social dominance in inbred mouse strains. *Nature,* 1961, 191, 474-476.

Polani, P. E. Occurrence and effect of human chromosome abnormalities. In L. Platt and A. S. Parkes (eds.), *Social and genetic influences on life and death.* London: Oliver & Boyd, 1967, pp. 3-19.

Sands, D. E., and Chamberlain, G. H. A. Treatment of inadequate personality in juveniles by dehydroisoandrosterone. *Brit. Med. J.,* 66-68, 1952.

Sano, K., Yoshioka, M., Ogashiwa, M., Ishijima, B., and Ohys, C. Posteromedial hypothalamotomy in the treatment of aggressive behaviors. *2nd International Symposium on Stereoencephalotomy, Vienna 1965, Confinia Neurologica,* 1966, 27, 164-167.

Santos, M., Sampaio, M. R. P., Fernandes, N. S., and Carlini, E. A. Effects of *Cannabis sativa* (marihuana) on the fighting behavior of mice. *Psychopharmacologia,* 1966, 8, 437-444.

Scott, J. P. Genetic differences in the social behavior of inbred strains of mice. *Journal of Heredity,* 1942, 33, 11-15.

Scott, J. P. *Aggression.* Chicago: University of Chicago Press, 1958.

Serafetinides, E. A. Aggressiveness in temporal lobe epileptics and its relation to cerebral dysfunction and environmental factors. *Epilepsia,* 1965, 6, 33-42.

Tedeschi, R. E., Tedeschi, D. H., Mucha, A., Cook, L., Mattis, P. A., and Fellows, E. J. Effects of various centrally acting drugs on fighting behavior of mice. *Journal of Pharmacology and Experimental Therapeutics,* 1959, 125, 28-34.

Telfer, M. A., Baker, D., Clark, G. R., and Richardson, C. E. Incidence of gross chromosomal errors among tall criminal American males. *Science,* 1968, 159, 1249-1250.

Tolman, J., and King, J. A. The effects of testosterone propionate on aggression in male and female C57BL/10 mice. *Brit. J. Anim. Behav.,* 1956, 4, 147-149.

Uyeno, E. T. Effects of D-lysergic acid diethlyamide and 2-bromlysergic acid diethylamide on dominance behavior of the rat. *International Journal of Neuropharmacology,* 1966a, 5, 317-322.

Uyeno, E. T. Hallucinogens and dominance behavior of the rat. *Proceedings of the Western Pharmacology Society,* 1967a, 10, 94. (Abstract)

Uyeno, E. T. Hallucinogens and dominance behavior of the rat. *Proceedings of the Internationales de Pharmacodynamie et de Therapie,* 1967b, 169, 66-69.

Valzelli, L. Drugs and aggressiveness. *Advances in Pharmacology,* 1967, 5, 79-108.

Washburg, S. L. One hundred years of biological anthropology. In J. O. Brew (ed.), *One hundred years of anthropology.* Cambridge: Harvard University Press, 1968, pp. 97-118.

Welch, J. P., Borgaonkar, D. S., and Herr, H. M. Psychopathy, mental deficiency, aggressiveness and the XYY syndrome. *Nature,* 1967, 214, 500-501.

Wiener, S., Sutherland, G., Bartholomew, A. A., and Hudson, B. XYY males in a Melbourne prison. *Lancet,* 1968, 1, 150.

Yen, C. Y., Stranger, R. L., and Millman, N. Ataractic suppression of isolation-induced aggressive behavior. *Archives Internationales de Pharmacodynamie et de Therapie,* 1959, 123, 179-185.